HEART OF UX

The Way of the Connected Researcher

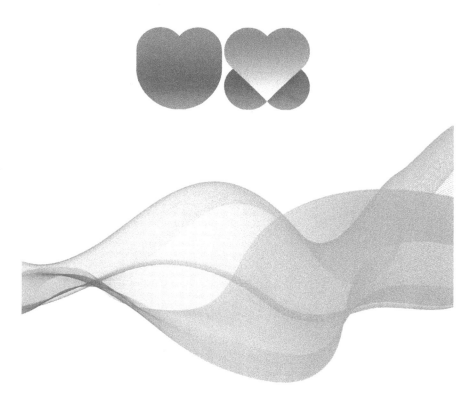

JESSICA STEINBOMER & JON-ERIC STEINBOMER

Cover image © Charles Hurst

Copyright © 2020 Progress User Experience Research

Kendall Hunt Publishing Company previously published this book.

ISBN: 978-1-7345034-1-8

All rights reserved. No part of this publication may be reproduced, stored in a retrieval system, or transmitted, in any form or by any means, electronic, mechanical, photocopying, recording, or otherwise, without the prior written permission of the copyright owner.

Printed in the United States of America

TABLE OF CONTENTS

FOREWORD... vii
PREFACE: FOLLOW THE LONGING xiii
INTRODUCTION: WHY THE HEART OF UX 1
WHO THIS BOOK IS FOR............................. 6

PART I: THE INGREDIENTS OF EMPATHIC CONNECTION . 9

THE NEUROSCIENTIFIC BASIS OF EMPATHY 11
    Creating Connections between People and Technology 11
    Situational Awareness............................ 11
    The Triune Brain 12
    How We Resonate 14
    The Neuroscience of Trust........................ 16
    The Neuroscience of Forgiveness.................. 18
THE HEART AS AN ORGAN OF PERCEPTION 24
    What's Love Got to Do with It?................... 24
    More Than a Muscle: HeartMath.................... 27
    To Cohere or In-Cohere 28
    Empathy in the Field of Heart Awareness 31
EMOTIONAL INTELLIGENCE AND EMOTIONAL AGILITY... 33
THE BODY SPEAKS...................................... 35
    Listening and Understanding One Another Through the Lens of the Body............................. 35
    The Vagus Nerve 36

PART II: THE HEART OF UX PRINCIPLES 41

THE HEART OF UX PRINCIPLES 43
PRINCIPLE ONE: POSITIVE PRESENCE.................. 44
    Presence to the Rescue........................... 44
    The ROI of Presence 45
    Something Out of Nothing......................... 48
PRINCIPLE TWO: MINDFULNESS 49
    An Introduction to Mindfulness................... 50
PRINCIPLE THREE: CONGRUENCE....................... 54
PRINCIPLE FOUR: FOLLOW ALIVENESS.................. 59

PRINCIPLE FIVE: SYNCHRONISM 61
PRINCIPLE SIX: RESOURCING. 63
   Self-Compassion 64
   The Four Noble Truths of Technology 66
   The Rift, or Suffering. 67

PART III: THE HEART OF UX TECHNIQUES 71
MASTERING THE ART AND CRAFT OF UX 73
THE BIG WHY 73
   Remembering Our Purpose. 74
EXPERIMENTAL ATTITUDE 75
ATTUNEMENT: BEYOND SOMEONE ELSE'S SHOES. 77
   Connection + Compassion = Attunement 77
ORIENTING. 78
REFLECTIVE LISTENING. 79
ATTUNED NOTICING 81
   Attuned Noticing as a Pathway to Meaning. 83
CONTACT STATEMENTS 85
   Contact vs. Leading 86
SAVORING THE GOOD 87
   Soul Nourishment. 88
   Finding Inspiration. 92
SELF-CARE AND THE ART OF LIVING. 94
   Artfully Seeing the Cycles of Life 95
ACTIVE RECEIVING/LISTENING. 97
   It's the Little Things 100
BOUNDARIES 100
   Clearing the Air 102
GOING OFF SCRIPT 103
UNCONDITIONAL POSITIVE REGARD 104
   Cultivating Unconditional Positive Regard. 106
   We Were All Kids Once 106
   UPR and Remote Research. 106
ETHICS AND RIGHT ACTION. 107
   Understand Your Values and Ethical Guidelines. 107
   The Responsibility of Power in Research 108
   Know Your Role 108

BRINGING IT ALL TOGETHER 109
PART IV: EMBRACING YOUR BIAS 111
EMBRACING YOUR BIAS 113
APPRECIATIVE INQUIRY: QUESTIONS ARE FATEFUL 113
    The Affirmative Question 114
    The Research on Word Choices 115
    The Basic AI Process: 5-D Model 116
    AI and UX Research 120
    Get Started with Positive Framing 121
THE INTENTIONAL OBSERVER EFFECT 122
    Behind the Looking Glass 124
    Clever Hans, Mind Your Hooves 124
    Schrödinger's Cat and Jakob Nielsen's Dog 126
    The Intentional Influence of Compassion 127
    Acknowledging Our Bias from the Beginning 128
    Bodily and Emotional Bias 129
PART V: RESEARCH FOUNDATIONS AND LOGISTICS . . . 131
BUILDING YOUR TEAM 133
    Stakeholders: Prime Movers of UX 133
    Determining the Needs of the Project 133
    Make Sure the Schedule and Scope Make Sense 134
STUDY PLANNING 134
    Components of a Study Plan 135
    Sharing the Study Plan 139
    Best Practices for Study Planning 139
MODERATOR'S GUIDES 140
    Components of a Moderator's Guide 140
CONDUCTING RESEARCH SESSIONS 142
    At the Start of Each Research Day:
    Cultivating the Curious Witness 142
    Before Starting Each Session—
    Pre-Session Checklist 142
    Participant Orientation 143
    After Ending Each Session—Post-Session Debrief
    and Release 145

VIDEO AND THE HEART OF UX.................... 147
   Embracing the Camera......................... 147
VIDEO MASTERY IN QUALITATIVE RESEARCH.......... 150
   Remote Research.............................. 151
   The in-person Usability Lab 154
   In The Field/On Location..................... 157
   In Focus Groups.............................. 159

A Final Word...................................... 163
Acknowledgments.................................. 167
About The Authors 169
Notes... 171

FOREWORD

Foreword

Foreword for Heart of UX
R. G. Bias

Professionals in the field of User Experience Design (UXD) employ a variety of methods as they help design artefacts – proven methods to gather data about users and potential users. Some methods enable us to gather data to drive "user requirements" to inform designs, and other methods allow us to gather data to evaluate emerging designs, to assess the excellence of the designed user experience.

One method we use is personas – characterizations of representative sub-populations of users and potential users of our designed products. There is variation in how UX professionals craft their personas, but common components include a name (so a team can say "Yes, 'Nancy' needs this feature"), often a picture, some demographic information (age, socio-economic status, perhaps education level, perhaps level of experience with predecessor or competitor projects), and maybe predicted context of use of the product under design (say, what device Nancy likely will be using).

Well, consider, if you will, the following three personas, NOT of potential product users, but of members of a product development team. Darcy, Jeremy, and Heather work for SatisfactoryApps, a small web-development company, and have been pressed for time (sound familiar?) to ship a new, transaction-based web app.

- Darcy, Director of development – 38 years old. BS in computer science and an MBA. Fifteen years of experience in software development. Recently hired in from a large enterprise software development company.
- Jeremy, UX team manager – 37 years old. BS in electrical and computer engineering, ex development manager who was shifted to the UX team because of his superior management skills.
- Heather, UX team member – 28 years old. BA in art history. Ex travel journalist who earned a well-known certification in UX and joined the company six months ago.

Darcy, Jeremy, and Heather and all the rest of the SatisfactoryApps team launched their app on time. And though it had met all the measurable usability criteria, and the team had followed good UXD practice, the app was a flop. How could this be? Heather employed a reasonable and imminently defensible set of UX methods during the design and development of the product. Jeremy is an award-winning manager, with an excellent history of good communication, upwards and down within an organization. And Darcy, well, she didn't get to be a director by age 38 by being lucky. She has serious software app development game, as many Fortune 500 companies who were customers of her earlier products would testify.

An important trait for designers, according to almost every article on design one reads today, is empathy. Empathy for the user. Empathy for the customer (who may be different from the user). Empathy for fellow developers.

So how did that perfect storm happen for SatisfactoryApps? Heather did carry out all the "right" UX methods, but her lack of empathy for her usability test participants meant she missed a bunch of important findings. She had conducted a heuristic evaluation, then just basically conducted the end-user testing as a way to confirm her findings. Jeremy, well established in the company and known for his management prowess, presented the UX results in an arrogant way and showed so little empathy for his audience – the dev team – that they did a relatively poor job of implementing Heather's recommended redesigns. Darcy with her years of experience in enterprise software development, demonstrated lack of empathy for the ultimate web app users, whose usability data didn't match her intuitions, thus leading her to not demanding more, and a more careful response to Heather's recommendations, and thus to shipping an on-time but inferior product.

In *Heart of UX* Jessica and Jon-Eric Steinbomer argue for the value of being a "Connected Researcher." Integrating such seemingly (but not) disparate topics as Zen Buddhism and neuroscience, soul nourishment and coherence, the Steinbomers proffer an approach that offers "a means of making technology more human-centric and more heart-centric for all of us."

Here are two fundamental questions about empathy:

1. Can empathy be taught, or is it just present (or not) congenitally, like red hair or left-handedness?
2. If it can be taught, how might it be taught?

In *Heart of UX* Jessica and Jon-Eric offer a hearty "yes" to question number one, and then spend about 200 clearly-written pages offering expert and tested techniques for how to teach, or cultivate one's own, empathy.

Foreword

In Part I the authors steep their offering in empiricism, including a section on the "Neuroscientific basis of empathy."

Before the specific methods presented in Part III, Part II presents the six Heart of UX principles, including, as you have read in the Table of Contents, such things as Mindfulness and Positive Presence. Peppered throughout this Part, and beyond, are exercises (e.g., "Reflective listening") and personal stories that represent in lovely, accessible ways the science and theory and method being described.

And thus to instantiate the six principles, Part III offers "specific and tangible techniques" to help the UX professional become a Connected Researcher.

Part IV is "Embracing your bias." UXD is a marriage of quantitative and qualitative methods. Almost any contemporary treatise on good qualitative practice acknowledges that the human researcher is an "instrument"; we cannot deny our individual differences, our different experiences and beliefs. Rather, we must strive to acknowledge them and understand them as the context in which we observe our test participants and indeed the whole world. In Part IV you'll receive much actionable advice on how to do just that.

Part V – Research Foundations and Logistics – provides a fundamental reference, interspersing a helpful checklist designed to help with "focusing on how to integrate the Heart of UX methods into your work with stakeholders." From hiring practices to camera placement to how the Connected Researcher should be positioned, physically, beside the person being researched, the authors have taken us from theory and research to some serious nuts-and-bolts how-to.

The discipline of design is at an inflection point, with much tardy attention being focused on the ethics of HCI design. For years we have attended to accessibility. The software development world is now (almost) universally aware of the need for those of us who are "temporarily able-bodied" to provide content and processes that are equally available to those with sensory/perceptual/motor challenges. We now, finally, have turned our attention to how our designs might unintentionally exclude people of a certain culture or race or gender or age. Heart of UX comes at this inflection point of our discipline, providing us with some explicit direction for how to treat all, even ourselves, with respect. Connected Researchers, we read, are in connection with themselves. "They wield empathic abilities that come with great responsibility, and they do so with a sense of ethics and genuine care for the customer, their team and the broader community . . . . As a culture, we are shifting from an aggressive and self-centered, dog-eat-dog world to one where we work together for the common good." Thank you, Jessica and Jon-Eric, for helping us along this path. "Darcy," "Jeremy," "Heather," and I, and indeed all of the users of our future designs, will reap the benefits of your efforts.

Just to be clear, I am not the "Bias" whom Jessica and Jon-Eric are talking of embracing, in their "Part IV – Embracing your bias." But I am pleased that they did embrace me, as their employer, 20 years ago, and again recently, when they invited me to write this foreword. In my 42 years of toiling (joyfully) in our usability/UX discipline, I have seen many broad approaches come and (sometimes) go. And I am proud to be associated with the Steinbomers' thoughtful, talented, integrative, empirically-based and overdue addition to our tool belt. Indeed, given their rich collection of empathy-stimulating methods, you and I may need yet an additional belt.

--

As I was writing this foreword I took a break and began reading the book Living Beautifully with Uncertainty and Change by American Buddhist nun Pema Chödrön. There I read, ". . . or we can relax and embrace the open-endedness of the human situation, which is fresh, unfixated, unbiased" (p. 14). This struck me as not only good instruction for living life, but fundamentally good advice for the UX professional who wishes to observe, evaluate, and ultimately serve users and potential users of the products and work flows that professional is helping design. Chödrön asks, "How do we get in touch with the fundamental ambiguity of being human in the first place?" One could ask the same about the fundamental ambiguity of being a UX professional, and many of the answers to this question of "how" are provided here by Team Steinbomer.

Randolph G. Bias
August 3, 2020

Chödrön, P. (2013). Living beautifully with uncertainty and change. Boston: Shambhala Publications.

PREFACE:
FOLLOW THE LONGING

Preface: Follow The Longing

JESSICA'S STORY

The Heart of UX is a byproduct of following my desire to live a fuller and more intimate life. It was 2014, and User Experience (UX) was a burgeoning field, defining and redefining itself all the time. During this time, I was co-leading a UX research company, work which required having vision, exercising oversight of projects, conducting research, analyzing and synthesizing complex problems, and managing a team. I could feel in all of my interactions that I carried a head-centric ambition; an attitude of perfectionism; a scientific rigidity that I thought made me legitimate; a disparity between the way I wanted to be in the world and how I was spending each day. Those days were filled with a repetition that was silently agonizing—and my approach was no longer satisfying. I was told that if I worked hard enough, I could one day stop working so hard, and then and only then, have fun. So I pressed on, driving toward a goal and paying the bills.

But I craved deeper connection above all else. Through a friend, I found a reason to enroll in a somatic, body-based therapeutic training from the Hakomi Institute. This seemingly had nothing to do with my work in research, but my heart led me to it and I couldn't say no. I secretly hoped it would lead me into a whole new life, to find higher ground and leave behind the reality I was experiencing.

The Hakomi Institute's somatic psychology training, called Hakomi Mindfulness-Centered Somatic Psychology, is named from a Hopi word meaning "how you stand in relation to all the realms." It is an intensely personal way of realizing intimacy with all things. It is used as a therapeutic method between therapists and clients to bring wholeness into lives by working with patterns and messages in the body. The Hakomi Institute explains these Principles[1] more fully.

"Integrating scientific, psychological, and spiritual sources, Hakomi has evolved into a complex and elegant form of psychotherapy that is highly effective with a wide range of populations. The method draws from general systems theory and modern body-centered therapies including Gestalt, Psychomotor, Feldenkrais, Focusing, Ericksonian Hypnosis, Neuro Linguistic Programming, and the work of Wilhelm Reich and Alexander Lowen. Core concepts of gentleness, nonviolence, compassion, and mindfulness evolved from Buddhism and Taoism.

At its most basic level, Hakomi is the therapeutic expression of a specific set of Principles: Mindfulness, Nonviolence, Unity, Organicity and Mind-Body Integration; these tenets inform every aspect of the work."[2]

During this training, my life, my career and my identity underwent a reformation, and I experienced reclamation of my purpose in the world. While conducting high profile studies and mentoring new researchers, I became curious about relating to people through the tools I had learned in Hakomi. A new way of being in the world was seeping into all aspects of my life like sweet, golden, raw honey. And it was good. I noticed that the UX study participants I talked to were now more relaxed, had greater trust, and more rapid rapport with me. They also were willing to offer me deeper vulnerabilities, which pointed me to their truer needs. I began to see myself not only as an instrument and voice of the people but as a resonance facilitator, a "needs intuitor" rather than a collector and regurgitator of opinions.

I also noticed during my training that the research results I delivered contained more depth, as well as more potent and courageous recommendations. I was giving the creative design teams a real, live, and embodied sense of their target user that they could feel first and then understand. People began to note that there was something different about the way I conducted the research sessions, something more alive and satisfying about the results. Our team became a cohesive group of close friends.

In the years since my training and the experience that flowed from it, I now offer our work as a way to bring disparity and separation together into a unified oneness. To live on the outside the same as you feel on the inside. To deepen in every connection, to nourish and offer compassion to yourself and others, to enjoy each moment as much as possible, and to live into an integrated wholeness. *The Heart of UX* shows how you can do the same. Bringing key principles from this book into a daily practice can enrich your life. Utilizing the empathic toolkit presented in this book, your research sessions will produce richer connections with study participants. Connection leads to joy—not the kind of joy that is subject to the waves of life, but a deep abiding joy. This joy leads to emotional agility and resonance between researcher and participant, which in and of itself provides a healing interaction.

Preface: Follow The Longing

At the heart of this practice, you and your participants feel refreshed and more alive after a study session than before it. This then provides profound data, which helps guide ideas and products. Systems evolve from a place of true need and true connection. You are literally tapping in to all of creativity, together, trusting the same creativity that birthed the universe. The opportunities that arise from the primordial sea of creativity now have a clear channel, from the research participants you engage with, to designers, creators, executive teams, and decision makers, and then circling back to those who were the source of your original data—the customers.

We are all in this together and can rely on this interconnected co-arising. As a culture, we are shifting from an aggressive and self-centered, dog-eat-dog world to one where we work together for the common good. Continuing to integrate our practice of wholeness into every interaction provides a way for us to live in bliss, and for organizations to profit ethically, while serving the needs of humanity. Refreshingly real research drives technology to serve humanity, while allowing us to enjoy our life fully.

JON-ERIC'S STORY

I've worked as a UX researcher since 1999, when Prince was still partying and Jakob Nielsen was spreading the good news about usability engineering. As a consultant for most of my career, I'm grateful for many opportunities to have worked intimately with a uniquely broad array of companies, primarily in the technology sector. I've helped experiences take shape for an equally diverse range of technologies: robotics, home automation, self-driving cars, e-commerce websites, apps, and services.

I've always been captured by an affection for technology that started when I was young. In 1983, when I was 11, I worked in the first store in Austin to sell Apple computers. Computers 'N Things was around the corner from my house. Because I was younger than the legal working age, they paid me in software in exchange for unboxing and setting up Apple IIe systems for people. In truth though, I would have easily worked there for free. I got to see first-hand what was then the cutting edge of consumer technology before anyone else. I powered up the first Mac computers the day they arrived in the store to great fanfare (the first computers to feature a mouse!) I used a telephone-based modem to talk with people across the world on bulletin boards. I play-tested a new video game that the store owner was developing in their spare time. I loved all of it.

Later in life, my fascination turned to a deep interest in people, when I took my first psychology course in high school. From that moment, I dreamed of being a clinical psychologist. When I went to college and majored in psychology, I was completely hooked. I was especially drawn to the study of neuroanatomy and the emerging findings in neuroscience. I worked with a postgraduate psychophysicist who was investigating the visual system. I interned in the psych department as their resident tech support staffer (those tech skills came in handy), and I spent a lot of time in the basement digging around in boxes of unused EEG equipment and MMPI testing manuals. After pursuing entrance to graduate school to begin my clinical studies, two things happened that changed my path with psychology completely: my discovery of Human Factors and the dot.com boom of the late 90s.

Human Factors is a branch of psychology that studies the interactions between people and machines. Discovering this field was a watershed moment for me. I didn't know it would be possible to couple my interests in technology and people into one cohesive career path. With the allure of working in this field immediately after graduating college, and filled with enthusiasm, I jumped ship from my grad school path and began my first internship as a usability engineer. After more than 20 years of work in the research business since then, I've still not lost the fascination with people and how they intermix with the technologies they create.

In addition to my work in the tech industry, I've also completed comprehensive training and/or practice with: Appreciative Inquiry, Hakomi Mindfulness-Centered Psychotherapy, Spiral Dynamics, the Inner View™ method of filmmaking, as well as a long-standing practice and study of mindfulness rooted in Zen Buddhism. All of these teachings attracted me as they have something in common—they center on how we relate and deepen with ourselves and one another. They have completely transformed my approach and interactions with research participants, stakeholders, colleagues—and people in general.

Integrating these practices directly into my work, I've found this relational skillset to be uniquely imperative in the tech sector, where deep insights derived by grounded, empirical qualitative research fuel innovation and transformation. Technology is everywhere, and it can be beautiful—especially when it elegantly, easefully serves people and meets their authentic needs, desires and aspirations. I and others believe this to be our ethos as user experience professionals and this book is an attempt to further ensure that people are at the heart of the user experience.

INTRODUCTION

Introduction

WHY THE HEART OF UX?

In the center of the Pacific Ocean, the Hawaiian Islands rise impressively from the surrounding vast blue waters. In the center of this archipelago chain sits Molokai, the island known to native Hawaiians as the Island of Powerful Prayers. It is one of the most lush, abundantly beautiful places on earth, surrounded by waterfalls and high sea cliffs. The prayers and dreams we've experienced there, both attending and leading multiple retreats, have focused our efforts and have helped our deepest work to surface. It has helped us to remember that connection is at the core of everything.

It is there, in the center of the center that this story begins. You see, the most powerful movements start from the center, and in the case of User Experience research, this is also true. At the very center of product development and design lies the practice of UX research. Research informs design and product teams about people's behaviors, desires, fears, and needs. It is the beating pulse of effective design, and is at the heart of all successful tech companies. Right at the center of UX research is what we call The Heart of UX—the ability to connect.

Why do we assert that connection is so central? Every tool, platform, piece of software, or hardware started in someone's mind as an idea and then took form as a design. This design's purpose is to make a connection. Whatever the purpose of the connection, to effect a purchase, persuade, inform, or entertain, it's a connection at its core, and in this arc of fulfillment between the idea and our usage, the design is given life, if only for a moment.

This is the basic relationship between the user and the experience that we colloquially condense as the User Experience, and like all relationships, it takes work to get it right. So how do we make connections that are both lasting and meaningful? The most direct path is through the skillful practice of UX research. It provides foundational, grounded evidence from which to design and develop experiences. Lacking this foundation, design can only be performed using best guesses and personal perspectives, rolling the dice and hoping things will work out—but we all know that great designs are rarely the result of chance.

There was a time not long ago when stating this assertion was met with substantial resistance. It felt like we were constantly trying to convince others of our legitimacy. With very little in the way of patterns to follow, over the last 20 years we as researchers have dreamed and grown a substantive craft of what we now know of as UX research. Working together from a place where almost no one knew what usability even was, now we're here: researchers from all over the world share a common confidence, culture, and lexicon around techniques, principles, and terminology.

Correspondingly, we've earned the respect of those within the walls of tech giants, many of whom rely on our empirically driven insights and as a result, boast robust teams of talented researchers.

While our hard work has earned us a well-deserved seat at the table, we wrote this book because the technology that is ever more a part of our lives is currently evolving in new directions we've only imagined possible. As a result, it's time for us as UX researchers to take the next step in our co-evolution. It's time we join together, level up, and forge a new path forward.

The Connected Researcher

We call this new path the way of the Connected Researcher. Who is a Connected Researcher? You may work with some of them already. They're people who are able to interview their research participants in a way that most people can't. They can sense when a person is experiencing a subtle frustration that belies their consciously spoken words. They can probe deeper into a person's outer narrative, finding the bits of their authentic personal truths that otherwise would lie undiscovered. They can sit with a person who may be anxious about being interviewed on camera and in front of a two-way mirror, and help calm them—intentionally co-regulating them with their own serene nervous system.

When you watch a Connected Researcher work, it's captivating. It's like watching a master artist at their craft, divining each next stroke of conversation from the formless field of possibility. The participants who they work with say things they would normally hold back, otherwise restraining themselves from fears of judgment or hurting someone's feelings with what they really think. Often the restraint comes from a fear of judgment or hurting someone's feelings with what they really think.

These researchers also take their unique skill sets outside the lab. The Connected Researcher is the most calming presence in the room. They know how to make contact with the leader of the development team and help her feel heard. They help the overclocked product manager remember to breathe in the midst of high stakes and a fast pace. All of these skills improve teamwork, innovation, and ultimately result in a much better product.

They also have a community. Researchers work together, united under a common goal of ensuring that people outside of the organization have a seat at the table in the design of the technology that is being co-created with and around them.

Most importantly, the Connected Researcher is in connection with themselves, linked to their own bodies, their own minds, and their own hearts. This connection to self is what really gives them what appear to be superpowers. They know when someone is saying something they don't actually feel comfortable saying because they can feel it, based upon their own experience. They wield empathic abilities that come with great responsibility, and they do so with a sense of ethics and genuine care for the customer, their team, and the broader community.

Although it may look like magic or some innate, relational gift, this level of mastery is completely attainable. After learning the skills and techniques presented in this book, and much practice, you will gain the knowledge and practical skill set to be a Connected Researcher.

Origins

The Heart of UX is a framework that will help you achieve greater connections in ways you may have never experienced before, as a researcher and in your life. It is based heavily on our many years of direct experience as UX researchers in the industry. It is also greatly informed by our ongoing studies and practices in interrelated teachings, some rooted in the disciplines of emerging neuroscience, others more empirical or spiritual. Some of the teachings you will see in this book (among others) are adapted from or influenced by:

- Hakomi Mindfulness-Centered Somatic Psychology
- A General Theory of Love
- Appreciative Inquiry
- HeartMath

- The works of Dan Siegel
- Flow States
- Zen Buddhism & Meditation

As researchers, we are not therapists. But we are tasked with being with people, lots of people, day in and day out. It is our job to hear people's stories and actively feel their pain and understand their perspectives. Some of the people we speak with may be struggling or going through difficult life events. We understand that empathy is much more than walking in the other person's shoes. Our hearts and lives are affected by the stories we hear, and the data we bring back to the product team. We know it is our job to convey these stories, not just about how someone couldn't find a product on a website, but their underlying motivations, needs, and unmet needs. To that end, we've also included resources in this book to provide the support and self-care you may find helpful on this journey of self-discovery.

We hope that you will use these skills as a means of making technology more human-centric and more heart-centric for all of us.

Let's begin.

WHO THIS BOOK IS FOR

Although this book is easily applicable to all who work with people, it is aimed at User Experience (UX) researchers and qualitative researchers at all career levels who are looking for techniques of deepening and purposefully connecting with research participants. It is a field-tested approach for refreshing and reinvigorating UX research for senior researchers and those with years of experience. It is also great for those new to UX research, professionals who are hoping to develop a solid set of interviewing techniques that will immediately amplify their skillset. *The Heart of UX* is also for people who might be interested in starting a career in UX research, as well as for product or design team members interested in UX or asked to perform UX research.

For the sake of clarity and scope of this book, we define a UX researcher as someone who is part of the development team for apps, web products, software, or services: basically anything involving technology, who acts as a conduit between the people who make products and the people who use them. These researchers are the voice of humanity and care for human needs in the product design process.

Qualitative UX researchers approach questions primarily by talking to people, either in person or remotely. They solve problems like:

- An e-commerce company is noticing a lot of people dropping off during check-out and they want to know why. A researcher would recruit these customers to have a conversation with them and then watch them select a product, place it in their shopping cart, and attempt to check out. They might notice that there's a problem with the check-out process or some other factor that's getting in the way of people completing the purchase. The researcher then assimilates this information, conducts analysis and synthesis, then provides recommendations to the client in order to help them fix the issue.
- Designers develop a prototype of a hardware device and want to know if people can use it. Researchers take the prototype into the lab with people before it is manufactured to save massive amounts of development dollars. Being able to authentically connect with someone is paramount in order to understand if this product is something that this person really wants and needs or if they are just being polite, just there for the research session compensation, or not interested.

Research saves companies billions of dollars, oodles of time, and prevents disappointment by pointing development and design in the direction of actual human needs and practical use.

People who read this book will gain:

- Clarified vision and creativity for designing better products.
- Increased connection with co-workers, study participants, and client teams.
- A greater sense of wholeness as a person.
- Enlivened purpose in your career.
- A way to connect to your work and world more deeply.
- Specific and reliable tools for empathy.
- A deeper understanding of how empathic connection enriches the data collection, as well as overall performance.

...ree pillars that hallmark the Heart of UX approach to UX research:

- A love of people.
- A desire to tell their stories.
- A drive to innovate how we do research.

If you also feel these things are important, this book is for you.

PART I
THE INGREDIENTS OF EMPATHIC CONNECTION

PART I: THE INGREDIENTS OF EMPATHIC CONNECTION

THE NEUROSCIENTIFIC BASIS OF EMPATHY

Creating Connections between People and Technology

Alive at the squishy, radiant core of this book is our desire to connect—to people, with people, to help other people connect to one another. It is a wholesome drive to live out loud and be openly, honestly, and fully mammalian: totally human. Our essential nature wants to connect. Our bodies, hearts, and minds yearn for it, we suffer when we are away from it, and we do radical things to get it, including pushing others away (what a paradox). This is a book about connection. It can and will happen all around us, all day every day, if we acknowledge that it is our most basic drive, our most essential desire, our inmost request, as Suzuki Roshi says. It will abound when you see this same wish in the people around you.

When you can see through the layers of things that keep us apart, straight to the core of each person and give them what they truly want—warm connection, a lightness of being, a wholehearted exchange—this becomes your real work in the world, under the surface of solving a design problem, or going the extra mile for that pay raise. From there, connection or lack of connection is all there is, all that exists, and the first and only problem to solve. Your ability to connect to the people who provide your data is at the core of the Heart of UX. And one of the main ways we connect is through our ability to feel and experience empathy. A basic definition of empathy is "the ability to sense other people's emotions, coupled with the ability to imagine what someone else might be thinking or feeling." Brené Brown, the renowned author and researcher who has focused her life's work on courage, vulnerability, and empathy takes the definition a step further. She says that "Empathy is communicating that incredible healing message of 'You're not alone.'"

Situational Awareness

Standing at the bar at a local coffee shop, I can hear and see people all around me connecting and communicating with each other. I overhear a group's mumbled conversation next to me, but I do not absorb the content as I stay in my own thoughts. Suddenly my attention focuses on them and

I realize that they are wondering where they will sit. My position at the bar prevents them from sitting next to each other, and I can change this. I move one seat down, and the problem is solved. But what caused me to shift my focus from my work, in the zone and generative, to the conversation next to me? There were at least 10 other concurrent conversations—why was this one special to my brain? Something happened in milliseconds that asked my attention to shift from what was going on within me, to what was going on around me. —Jessica

---

Empathy is a complex equation of input, stimulus, conditioning, and response. It happens all at once and within our whole system simultaneously. How we perceive the world around us and connect to others has many complex parts, so we begin at the top, with our brains.

The Triune Brain

The triune brain is a model of the evolution of the vertebrate forebrain and behavior, proposed by the American physician and neuroscientist Paul D. MacLean. It proposes that our brains are composed of three parts: the brain stem (reptilian brain), the limbic brain (mammalian), and the cortex. "The cerebral cortex plays a role in just about every neural process, like memory, perception, attention, awareness, consciousness, thought, language, problem-solving, advanced motor functions, and social abilities" The cortex, (primarily the forebrain), is given the responsibilities of higher processing, language, reason, and voluntary movement. The brain stem, our reptilian brain, is responsible for all of the basic functions of having a body: heart rate, breathing and all involuntary movement. The limbic brain envelops the brainstem and is surrounded by the cortex.

In our family, we have a saying that our daughter authored when she was a baby. "I'm the pickle in the middle of a love sandwich," she'd say as we wrapped our arms around her, surrounding her with our warm parental love. This is precisely the case for the limbic area of the brain—it is the pickle in the middle of a love sandwich.

The limbic system, caringly sandwiched between the fore and hind brain, is where attachment happens. The limbic brain is the seat of communion, maternal feelings, play, and love. Evolutionarily, mammals developed the limbic brain as they broke off from the reptiles; we see this in the way that mammals care for their young. A mother coos to her child to calm him, and a child's cry is an immediate and primal message to a mother's body to respond.

Composed of four parts, the limbic system works closely with the brainstem to give us our basic drives and emotions. This area of the brain is always evaluating our surroundings and helping us move towards pleasant experiences, and away from dangerous ones. The amygdala, one of the four parts of the limbic system, is particularly responsible for the fear response which is key for our survival. Highly emotional states can be created here, and we can act on them without awareness. In some cases, this enables us to survive, like jumping away from a coiled snake, or it can cause us to do things we later regret. In studies where patients have damaged amygdalas, we see diminished fear response and greater risk taking behaviors.

Resting atop the limbic system, the cortex surrounds the limbic brain. This area of the brain, in particular the prefrontal cortex, is involved in integration. In order to understand, process, and regulate the emotions created by the lower brain (limbic) we need the executive functioning of the prefrontal cortex. In his book *Mindsight*, Dan Seigel gives a thorough and up-to-date explanation of how understanding our neural make up helps **to prevent** us from "flipping our lid."[3] Essentially, it is the job of the prefrontal cortex to integrate all of the underlying parts of the brain, and serve as a regulatory center. As shown in the diagram below, we can understand a basic model of the brain by taking a look at our hand, and superimposing a simple model of the brain onto it. At the base of our hand and wrist, we imagine the brainstem and spinal cord. As you fold your thumb inside your hand, the thumb region represents the limbic system. Now wrap your fingers down around the thumb, creating the cortical layer. In this easy hand model of the brain, Dan explains that the middle prefrontal cortex, represented by the two middle fingers of our hand are particularly important in integration. This region of the brain helps to regulate the nervous system, gives us the ability to connect with others, allows for response flexibility (the ability to pause before responding), and the ability to calm fear. Through neurochemicals and hormones, the prefrontal cortex assists the other more primitive layers of the brain in maintaining calm, clear thought and action. As Dan explains, if you lift your fingers and then put them back down again, you will see the unique nature of this area of the brain—it helps to connect everything. So what happens when we

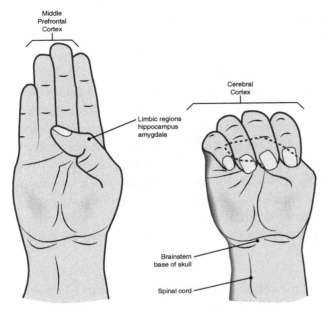

get dysregulated, or flip our lid? When we lose control of our behavior, and we all know what this feels like, we can end up acting in ways that we later regret. This is flipping our lid. So how do we keep from flipping our lid, from flying off the handle? And more importantly, what does this tell us about how we can best perform our work as Connected Researchers?

How do we foster, from within our own subjective experience, the ability to truly feel another person's experience of the world? Or in the case of damage or trauma, how do we lose these abilities? We'll come back to the prefrontal cortex in our section on mindfulness. But first, let us consider the elements that make up a healthy brain's experience of love, and see how that relates to connection, within and outside of qualitative research. There is a rapidly expanding body of research from neuroscientists, psychologists, and psychiatrists (like Dan Siegel) that allows us to form our discussion and inquiry into the ways we connect and feel empathy as human beings. As a Connected Researcher we can understand the science behind our minds, and engage in techniques and practices that amplify empathic connection. We can train and encourage the parts of our brains that have insight and behave in ethical ways to bring about a wholesome and enjoyable life. Let's take this bit one step further into how we actually feel each other's experience.

How We Resonate

Throughout the brain, there are special groupings of cells called mirror neurons that are responsible solely for feeling the feelings of another mammal.[4] These mirror neurons act like antennae between us. They transmit and receive experiences between living beings. We are constantly sending out signals into our environment. We can think of these signals as musical notes, vibrating at their own frequencies.

When we're walking around in the world, within our own experiences and perhaps lost in thought, these notes contribute to the sound and song of all emotional experiences of those who are around us. When we are with someone in mindful presence, however, these notes begin to entrain to one another and a harmonic is formed, a resonance. This is why, without even knowing about the brain's inner workings, we commonly say things like "we were on the same wavelength."

Thomas Lewis, Fari Amini, and Richard Lannon wrote in *A General Theory of Love*, "Within the effulgence of their new brain, mammals developed a capacity we call limbic resonance—a symphony of mutual exchange and internal adaptation whereby two mammals become attuned to each other's inner states."

Limbic resonance is the idea that the capacity to share deep emotional states arises in the limbic system. These states include empathic harmony, as well as fear, anxiety, and anger.

Much of limbic resonance happens all on its own, subconsciously. However, when we become not only aware of this resonance but utilize our sensate feeling of resonance to build rapport, we gain trust with a participant, client, or co-worker. Utilizing the techniques found later in this book, you will become aware of limbic resonance and how it feels in the mind and body. And you will wield your new abilities with agility and ease during research sessions, client meetings, interactions with coworkers, and the like. Because we are all mammals, we all require connection and resonance to thrive. Therefore, offering the gift of harmonious connection elevates not only our own experience, but all of those we interact with.

> *"Each time we meet another human being and honor their dignity, we help those around us. Their hearts resonate with ours in exactly the same way the strings of an unplucked violin vibrate with the sounds of a violin played nearby. Western psychology*

> *has documented this phenomenon of mood contagion or limbic resonance."*
>
> —Jack Kornfield,
> *The Wise Heart: A Guide to the Universal Teachings of Buddhist Psychology*

Knowing, or the awareness of our own internal states, is power. When we can witness what is happening—for example, as we observe our heart beating faster, we know we may be experiencing stress. We may also notice a change in our own physiological response as another feels joy. All of this is good data, beyond what is being said. We show (with our bodies) not tell (with our stories).

In the aforementioned experience in the coffee shop, I could feel the tension between the people looking for seating. The cues that registered in my limbic system were based on the people's tone, pace of talk, plus an uneasiness or a hesitation. These things were felt, not heard directly; no one said, "I'm frustrated!" However, my limbic system and nervous system picked up on the subtleties. We are picking up these cues daily, moment by moment. In fact, we are so often overwhelmed by information that we block out most of these cues. The practice offered here is to start to play with purposefully allowing your awareness to feel what other people are feeling in an experimental way.

The next time you are at a coffee shop, or public area, actively notice the other people around you. Now, allow your body some space to talk to you. Can you feel any subtle sensations that may be related to how the others in the room are feeling?

The Neuroscience of Trust

For more than a decade, neuroscientist Paul Zak and his team conducted research to answer the question, "Why do people trust each other?"[5] He hypothesized that there must be some neurological signal that helps us determine when to trust someone. In order to test this hypothesis, Zak and team designed an experiment that involved sending and receiving money.

In the experiment, a person chooses to send a certain amount of money to a complete stranger, with the added knowledge that the money will triple in amount once the recipient receives it. The recipient then has the choice to keep all of the money, or share it with the sender. The conflict is one of trustworthiness—will the recipient be trustworthy and share the spoils, or keep it all to himself?

Many of us have heard of oxytocin, the brain hormone responsible for bonding between a mother and child, aptly named the love hormone. This chemical is produced in, yes, you guessed it, the limbic system (specifically, the hypothalamus for all you brain geeks.) Resonance, and trust, is a result of a largely chemical process. Oxytocin also increases a person's empathy. Empathy and trust all come down to, at least in the brain, the hormone oxytocin.

The team discovered that the more money people received (denoting trust on the part of the sender) the more oxytocin their brain produced. And the amount of oxytocin the recipients produced predicted how trustworthy they would be in turn. The brain chemical was found to be involved in inviting and eliciting trust between strangers.

The team then set out to uncover and identify promoters and inhibitors of oxytocin. They found that stress is the number one inhibitor of oxytocin. When a person's system is under stress, perhaps from a difficult experience with technology, they are not as capable of interacting as well with others as they would be if their system is not under stress. Enter the typical usability lab, where classically we have two-way mirrors, cameras, and an unfamiliar environment. Left unaddressed, this lab environment often produces a stressed or hyperaroused response within the participants' systems.

It is widely known that stress upon the system inhibits performance, thereby affecting data collection. What we can deduce is that the data collected in these more stress-filled environments will differ from data collected in a more comfortable, natural setting. Sitting on your couch at home is a far cry from a usability lab in a nondescript brown building with no windows, a place where people you don't know watch you do something new.

So if the data quality is questionable and everyone's stressed and unhappy with the whole testing experience, what are we doing with our days, years, and lives?

The research further showed that *recognition* has the largest effect on trust. When we recognize, hear, and see deeply the internal motivations, feelings, and concerns of another person, we gain their trust. We recognize, by listening deeply, the underlying meaning and gain insight into that person's world. We also recognize the notion of a common humanity, a unity.

It is clear that when a person feels seen by another, when they are heard and understood by a kind observer, they trust more. Gaining trust leads to a deeper rapport, and a more meaningful interaction. When interviewing people for their product desires while observing their behaviors, you can connect to a person in a more meaningful way.

Using skills learned from the Heart of UX approach will not only give you permission to trust your own desire to have more meaningful connections, but will provide tried and true skills for eliciting trust. A simple formula then becomes: more meaningful interactions lead to better data.

Like a musician who plays by ear, a Connected Researcher intuits the needs of the participant, based on observable behaviors and interactions. She then asks, and affirms that her gut instinct is correct, not by leading, but by showing how deeply she is tuned in to that person and hearing them completely. Getting to the root of the desire, the unconscious action behind the behavior and the truest need for that participant helps point us to make recommendations that are more universally true and far-reaching. Through our work as researchers, we can then design products that are intuitive and clean, and serve a broader section of humanity.

The Neuroscience of Forgiveness

We have all experienced that flush of the face, that rise of heat and energy in the body that comes from a feeling we know as anger. When our systems feel flooded with such a strong emotion, we can break it down into physical and chemical processes in the body, to stories and beliefs and values that we hold in the mind, as well as feelings associated with the heart. As the anger rips through our system, we are often overwhelmed by the first, strongest feelings and must ride the waves of sensation. If we are growing in wisdom and maturity, we often know in some recessed place within us that our words and actions must be managed so as not to do more harm.

Road rage is an excellent example that we can all understand if we are honest. All of us who drive, at least. We know, for example, that the aggressive soccer mom that just barreled down on us and prevented us from entering the freeway, and nearly drove us off the road and killed all of our children as well as her own, must be punished. No. Wait. We know that it is *not* right to chase her down, that's what we meant to say. To chase her down and slip in front of her and slam on the brakes would possibly destroy other people as she careened carelessly into the back of us, ahem, setting off a chain reaction. So in the heat of the moment you can let off a little steam and flip her off in front of your children, or you can practice forgiveness, or both.

We meet these challenges every day. Some, as in the car example, are fast and fleeting, and others have a residue that keeps them around for a long time.

The truth is, staying angry is more detrimental than we think. Studies have shown that the long term effects of enduring anger, resentment, and vengeance are detrimental to our health. (Gordon et al., 2009; Seybold et al., 2001).[6] Conversely, people that practice forgiveness have decreased depression, anxiety and anger levels.

But how is forgiveness relevant to our state of mind as a researcher? As a whole, our overall sense of well-being is affected by many factors, both inside and outside of the work environment. We are the culmination of our experiences, our upbringing, and our conditioned way of seeing the world. You are what you eat, both physically, energetically, mentally, and figuratively. So, of course, as we move through the world, we take our stuff with us. As we gather data through talking and interacting with people, we are carrying our own baggage: the argument with our teacher, the time our aunt forgot to pick us up as a second grader. You get the picture. We can carry these things, adding them to our bodies like layers of clothes, heavier with each addition. We can wear these unforgiven experiences as a dirty lens, coloring and clouding our view.

An experienced researcher already knows to check their world view often, to see ways that bias, prejudice, and ignorance are informing the data collection as it filters through our brains. A Connected Researcher not only recognizes their world views, but also their own emotional and bodily states. If we are holding a grudge, or letting a hard interaction play over and over in our minds, we become distracted, distant, and disconnected. This is not to say that the ideal state is one of an unfeeling automaton. We begin by being human, just as we are and acknowledging our shortcomings, but we also allow the kindness of forgiveness to be experienced as well. Then and only then can we offer it to others and wipe the slate clean. And a clean slate, tabula rasa, is a good data collecting state indeed.

You may know the old story that goes like this:

One evening an old man told his grandson about a battle that goes on inside people. He said, "My son, the battle inside us all is between two wolves. One is corrupt. It is anger, envy, jealousy, sorrow, regret, greed, arrogance, self-pity, guilt, resentment, inferiority, lies, false pride, superiority, and ego. The other is virtuous. It is joy, peace, love, hope, serenity, humility, kindness, benevolence, empathy, generosity, truth, compassion, and faith."

The grandson thought about it and then asked his grandfather, "Which wolf wins?"

The old man simply replied, "The one you feed."

So how do we move from harsh feelings into compassion authentically and not just because we should do so? How do we keep a connection with others while not abandoning or denying our own experience? For example, how do we let go of the grudge we are holding against Bobby for not finishing his part of the project on time and getting it over to us so we can add our part?

One way that people cultivate compassion, for ourselves as well as others, is to practice a Loving Kindness meditation.[7] Loving Kindness meditation gives us a bridge, a path, and a tried and true method to help us move from our difficult experience of a person to the experience of understanding the world of that other person. This is not just "do it to be a good person" reasoning. Brain imaging studies[5] of people who practice loving-kindness meditation have been shown to have enhanced signals from regions of the brain associated with empathy, such as the amygdala. These are the very same regions that neuroscientists have shown to be *hypoactive* in people who lack empathy. The amygdala evaluates things in the environment to determine their importance—whether the value is positive or negative—then creates emotional responses to the stimuli considered important. It might also consolidate memories that have a strong emotional component, regardless of whether the associated emotions are pleasant or unpleasant.

Neurologically speaking, then, the best way to avoid becoming like the person who harmed you is to act compassionately—forgive them. Or in other words, exercise and utilize the areas of the brain that can see a wider perspective. Neuronal pathways are formed by repetition and neurons that fire together, wire together. As an example, when we need to memorize the bones in the body, we write them down on flashcards and practice over and over again with our friends. You can imagine an old stagecoach, riding through years of rainy seasons, carving out a well-worn groove. Loving Kindness, which helps make space for forgiveness, is also like this. The more we practice offering kindness to people, the more we emphasize the neuronal pathways that can be used to access forgiveness when necessary. We train the "muscle" of forgiveness, so that when the moment comes, that pathway is accessible, familiar, and at the ready. And the more we forgive, the more we perceive—we can see a bigger picture for our own lives, and therefore see others more clearly.

When we practice Loving Kindness meditation, it gives us an accessible and easy thing to do from just about anywhere to help us get back into an open state of coherence and flow. Even as a work-alone consultant, the practice of forgiveness through Loving Kindness (also known as metta), helps keep us on track, keeps client interactions healthy and positive, and keep minds clear for the task at hand. And this kind of person is much more trustworthy and accessible than the Dr. Jeckel part of ourselves that holds onto wrongdoings.

Victor Frankel survived three years of the most incomprehensible suffering while imprisoned in Nazi concentration camps. He wrote in *Man's Search for Meaning*, "Everything can be taken from a man but one thing, the last of the human freedoms—to choose one's attitude in any given set of circumstances, to choose one's own way."

Exercise: Metta (Loving Kindness Meditation) Practice

This practice will become a trusted tool in your Connected Researcher tool kit, as ubiquitous as duct tape is to, well, everything. Practicing metta gives you something to do when all you can do is think about how that last participant completely lied during recruiting and was the "wrong use case." Metta paves the mental road for reconnection to your own flow states, and therefore your ability to be present. Metta offers someone kindness, whether or not they deserve it, thereby ushering in feelings of forgiveness. And this frees you from the oppression of "stinkin' thinkin."

There are variations in how to practice Metta - this is the method as taught by Peg Syverson, and Flint Sparks.

Find a comfortable seat. Whether on a chair, or seated on the floor, make sure that your body feels supported and at ease. Close your eyes or let them be heavily lidded, allowing a small sliver of light.

Turn your awareness inward, or in other words, allow your inner experience to become clearer than your outer experience. Continue to soften the eyes. When you feel ready, dedicate to offering metta by internally repeating the phrases below.

First, picture someone you love very dearly. Imagine them standing right in front of you. See them smiling at you, feel them loving you. Now imagine you are saying these words to them:

May your body be at ease
May your heart be open
May your mind be boundless
May you awaken

Notice what it feels like in your body to offer these kind words to the person that you love. Notice any sensations in your chest and in your shoulders. Notice your face. Notice your hands. Watch as this good feeling washes over you.

Now bring to mind someone who is neutral in your life. You can think of a person at the grocery store, or a participant, someone you don't know very well. Now imagine you are saying those words to them.

May your body be at ease
May your heart be open
May your mind be boundless
May you awaken
Keep noticing and returning your attention to your body.

Now bring to mind someone that you are having difficulty with. Pay attention to the sensations in your body as you see this person's face arrive in your mind's eye. Now, as you are ready, offer those words again, to them.

May your body be at ease
May your heart be open
May your mind be boundless
May you awaken

Offer these words internally to yourself, right now, the person who is having this experience.

May your body be at ease
May your heart be open
May your mind be boundless
May you awaken

Now see all three people gathered in a circle, with you in the circle too. Offer the phrases to the whole circle.

May our bodies be at ease
May our hearts be open
May our minds be boundless
May we all awaken together

Notice how you feel. Can you feel a little bit of space around the thoughts of that difficult person that weren't there before? What is the quality of your presence now that you have offered loving kindness to yourself and others?

As a result of more compassion and loving kindness, creativity makes its home in your life. It all relies on your ability to open, connect, perceive through the heart's open window and allow the light in. When you learn to practice metta, over time your ability to stay connected and kind to clients, participants, and coworkers increases. And this is good business and good research.

THE HEART AS AN ORGAN OF PERCEPTION

What's Love Got to Do with It?

What if we told you that you could fall in love with every person you meet? Participants, co-workers, bosses, clerks, your accountant? What happens as you read that for the first time? Do all of the people who you don't want to fall in love with rise up in your mind? Do all of the ideas of what you don't want, how messy that would be, come barreling toward you like bulls destined to trample you for such thinking? These thoughts are practical, protective, and useful. We don't want to annihilate them, just get familiar with them. What is their origin? Where are the barriers to love? What do they look like and feel like? How thick or thin are they?

You may ask why we must know. It's because we build these walls to protect ourselves—to avoid the ultimate truth that we will lose people, and we mistake that with losing love. We build a wall that says "not that person" or "not right now" or "I don't deserve it" or "they'll hurt me." These all might be true, but why? Not what, but why? We think we know the answer, because it's our mind's job to solve problems. Remember our lovely discussion about the prefrontal cortex. The mind makes the answer, but the barriers to love reside in the heart. As we learn that the heart is an organ of perception, we begin to redefine the ways we understand.

As we think about it colloquially, the heart is an actual organ, as well as a place that is often thought to be a seat of many of our feelings. But what if there was a third and higher function of the heart? What if, like a radio receiver, the heart is actually our instrument of perceiving our truest highest state of being? And what if this being-ness is actually an internal joy that has no opposite? Then it would behoove us to uncover this joy, as well as the ways we block it and reason against it. It would benefit our lives to study why we keep it at bay—and how opening the perception of the heart leads to a richer life, deeper connections, problem-solving skills, and yes, better data.

The heart is a spacious place, and when our body-minds are fueled with spaciousness, there is fertile ground for growth, creativity, and new ideas. There's another way of saying this: when you learn to feel into your own intuition and trust yourself, you become more confident and as a result can listen more fully, more instinctually to others. The better you can clarify your own signal, the better quality signal you will recognize on the outside.

> ***"And now here is my secret, a very simple secret: It is only with the heart that one can see rightly; what is essential is invisible to the eye."***
>
> —*The Little Prince*

When we first identified and began utilizing the Heart of UX approach in research sessions, something shifted. Instead of trying to just get data, we began to see each person as an inspiration. From a place of presence, we could see that each person was a wellspring of beauty, depth, and ingenuity. We began to enjoy the research sessions, gleaning richness and a truer quality of connection from each interaction. By seeing each person as an inspiration, we invite an experience of a "flow state" into the conversation.

What is a flow state? As described by the renowned psychologist who was the first to name and study the phenomena, Mihaly Csikszentmihalyi, flow is the pleasurable experience of "a complete focusing on the task at hand—thus leaving no room in the mind for irrelevant information." It's the feeling of being in synchronicity with your experience and your work, when time slips away and "one is able to forget all the unpleasant aspects of life."[8] Research has shown that when jazz musicians are in a state of flow, the areas of the prefrontal cortex related to self-evaluation are inhibited.[9] Simultaneously, other areas of the cortex that experience pleasure are enhanced. Similarly, when athletes are in a state of flow, they can outperform their own best records with ease and grace, noticing the steady one pointed focus that comes from this specialized state of being. When we are in a flow state, we are creative, expansive, and efficient - we are optimized. But how does this apply to research and interviewing people?

Is it possible to feel flow with another person? You may recall times when you stayed up all night talking to a new friend, so engaged in the conversation that all perception of time slipped away and before you knew it, it was four a.m. and you wondered how you got there but you didn't care because it was so engaging. We're not saying that every research interaction will be this stimulating, but what we are asserting is that it's not only possible, but with the intention to do so and real-world practice with the techniques presented in this book, it's a much more likely occurrence. How much more enjoyable would your research be if you could experience it in this way? What other benefits may also be found with this kind of expansive, flow-inducing interaction?

We posit that this kind of interaction is where ideas happen, where our minds are freed from their well-worn groove of repetitive thinking and the field of possibility widens, more free to explore, deepen, and create something unique by integrating new ideas with those previously held. Creativity is always a recombinatory state—a new idea combining with a familiar or known idea to form something completely different.

Being able to widen the field of possibility and dance between thoughts is fundamental to creativity. The ability to design and develop products that are useful and engaging to the point of indispensability requires us to do no less than channel genius. Most UX designers and UX researchers decided on this career to make the world a better place, one experience at a time. In order to do this, we must be able to access the vast array of life, the infinite space of creative potentiality. In flow states, we invite this sense by living as if every interaction is meaningful, synchronistic, and valuable, "where consciousness is harmoniously ordered" as Csikszentmihalyi tells us. We pursue each moment for the sake of that moment, endeavoring to live life to the fullest.

As we discuss in the next section, when we invite the participation of the heart into our work, our body/mind systems begin to function together in one resonant, optimized, and amplified state. Our head, heart, and hands begin to work together in a congruent way. Instead of seeing a tangled problem to solve, we train ourselves to summon flow states by actively perceiving through the heart, in addition to our brains. We train up our abilities and build a practice around finding creativity, productivity, and inspiration in as many situations as possible. We've certainly found that this is a more efficient, effective, and sustainable way to get the job done.

As nourished and connected researchers who can engage with people at this energetic, integrated level of relating, we can now provide product teams with trustable, reliable, and human-centric recommendations that come from a positive, growth-oriented foundation of empirical research data. And that's how we create a better world, one conversation at a time. So lean in, open yourself to the possibility of an engaging, expansive conversation and get curious to discover what's most alive for the participant. It may not be on the script, but it might inspire something that's new, unique, and addresses a need at a core-level, issuing forth a product or service that has a huge impact on the world.

More Than a Muscle: HeartMath

Before we go further into exploring the field of the heart, let's take a moment to pause and reflect on why we feel this exploration is so central to this work. As qualitative researchers, the greatest instrument of measurement and understanding is our very own body. In fact, there is a longstanding understanding of this within the world of qualitative research—the concept of "researcher as instrument." This idea is not new necessarily, but it is a unique and an unusual juxtaposition to the commonly held ideas of an objective truth "out there" that deems measure with similarly external instrumentation. We're showing you how, specifically to work with the body as the primary instrument of data collection. To do so, we must again return to the heart of the matter.

To our knowledge, there is no greater authority on the emerging science of the relational properties of the heart than the aptly named HeartMath Institute. Nestled deep within the Redwoods in Boulder Creek, California, the HeartMath Institute has demonstrated that many of the intuitive views of the heart as the seat of intuition have clear physiological correlates. Since 1991, they have conducted extensive, rigorous research into the inner and outer workings of the heart and as a result, have developed tools and technologies that help people improve emotional well-being and optimize their performance. As qualitative researchers, leveraging these tools can only help us to trust ourselves and our built-in intuitive systems as a means of primary data collection.

Our hearts are faithful powerhouses, thumping and oscillating in the dark beneath our chests, every moment of every day of our lives. We know it to be composed of musculature and specialized chambers, squeezing and releasing in elegant coordination. And we know that it is intimately linked to the brain, occupying the most innervated connections between any two major organ systems. We may believe that most of these innervated conversations are top-down, with the brain dictating the next actions of the heart, but this is the opposite of what the science of neurocardiology is showing us. It turns out that the heart sends more neuronal signals to the brain than the brain sends to the heart.[10] Incredibly, recent discoveries in neurocardiology are showing us that the heart has its own intrinsic nervous system—one that makes decisions based on data that is sensed, processed, and perhaps even remembered.[11] It's clear that the brain and the heart are in constant communication with one another. The heart communicates with the brain and body in distinct ways, according to the HeartMath Institute: neurological, biological (biochemical and biophysical), and through electromagnetic communication. We will also see later that the vagus nerve is a major highway in the heart-brain interplay, but for now let's keep our attention on the heart and its role in the subtle field of intuition.

To Cohere or In-Cohere

One of the key discoveries made early on by HeartMath was the genius in unlocking a little-known metric, Heart Rate Variability (HRV): a measure of the interval between heartbeats. This gap between heartbeats varies. The Autonomic Nervous System (ANS) is constantly adjusting the heart rate, with the Sympathetic Nervous System speeding it up and the Parasympathetic Nervous System slowing it down. When these systems are in coherence with one another, the

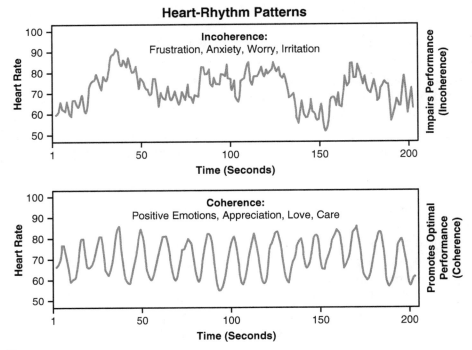

HRV is seen as a smooth sine wave. When incoherent, the outcome is a jagged plot of irregular peaks and valleys.

The experience of coherence in the body can be thought of as an optimal state where all systems are flowing together as designed, with precision and in coordination with one another.[12] Among other results, it produces optimal mental clarity, composure, effectiveness, and a positive mood and attitude. Things seem possible, the world is a safe and friendly place, and events just seem to flow from one to the other. The heart is actually an aperture where wisdom, intuition, and intelligence can be accessed to live with more balance, greater creativity, and increased personal effectiveness. This is an optimal state for research and design. We move about the world with efficiency, a powerful presence with an eye toward care. We are able to stay on schedule and collect deep insights at the same time, harnessing the potent force of an optimal human instrument.

Being in a state of incoherence is conversely related to feelings of anger, anxiety, and stress. Mental capacities are hindered as the body moves closer to survival mode and resources are diverted to possible fight or flight. As we saw previously, not only is our brain affected by anger, resentment and anxiety, but our hearts as well.

There's a very quick way to experience coherence right now, using your breath and following the Quick Coherence® Technique, developed by the HeartMath Institute.[13]

> Take a moment and turn your attention to your breathing. Without changing anything, just notice it, follow it. Now intentionally breathe in for five seconds and breathe out for five seconds while imagining the breath flowing in and out through your chest area. Next, actively cultivate feelings of appreciation. Think of a person, a place, or a beautiful place you can easily appreciate or feel gratitude for having in your life. Follow this practice for as long as it feels interesting—at least a full minute. What do you notice?
>
> You may experience a slowing of thoughts, a release of tension, perhaps even some enhanced awareness. Deliberately breathing in this way entrains your heart with the breath pattern and your heart/mind system enters coherence. This is an immediately and always-available tool to draw on when you feel you need it.

The most approachable method of sustaining this coherent state, right alongside everything else you may be doing in that moment, is to simply intend to evoke feelings of gratitude and appreciation. It may sound overly simple, but the science on this is well-known and reliably repeatable.[14] In the field of neurocardiology, scientists have discovered that the heart has a complicated and unique system of nerves, so subtle and profound that it has been given the name "the heart brain."[15] This heart brain gives the heart its own ability to make decisions, respond to environmental changes and offer wisdom, much like we read about in classical literature. Research has also revealed that the heart produces chemicals and neurotransmitters that affect the entire system. Yes, our old friend oxytocin is making another appearance here, as we confirm what we know in our hearts (pun intended). The ability to love and bond is also alive and well in the center of our chest, in our physical and metaphorical heart.

Scientists at UC Berkeley hypothesized that a daily practice of gratitude would have an effect on the overall wellbeing of subjects, and they were right. Out of 300 participants, three groups were formed. All three groups were diagnosed with depression and anxiety, and they received counseling services. One group was asked to commit to a daily practice of gratitude by writing a letter of gratitude to another person every day; another group was asked to write solely about their negative emotions; and the third group just received counseling. Those who wrote a letter of gratitude a day reported significantly better mental health for twelve weeks after the writing exercise ended.[16]

If you need more evidence, consider this scenario. A police sergeant with a team of heavily armed SWAT officers close behind him stealthily approaches a house that's about to be raided. The sergeant slowly raises his gloved hand, and with his gun at the ready and body armor secure, he gives a subtle signal. What happens next? The officers pause where they are. At this hand gesture, these men and women remember their gratitude training and invoke a feeling of thankfulness. They connect with something that makes them feel appreciation or gratitude, like the face of their child, a beautiful place, a precious memory. A few seconds later, they shift to visualizing an outcome for this operation in its best-case scenario for all persons involved. Through appreciation and imagining a best-case scenario, the officers align with themselves and each other through a sense of unified purpose and unequivocal kindness for all beings. Moments later, the sergeant abruptly drops his arm and they all follow in a phalanx behind the lead officer's shield as they rush forward, kick down the door and conduct the raid on the house. The operation is conducted expertly and no one is injured or killed. The suspects are arrested and taken into custody without incident.

In response to what was an unacceptable level of injuries and fatalities, several police forces around the world began teaching these same coherence techniques to their officers, and the results have been impressive.[17] Officers are more resourced, better able to quickly process situational information, less reactive, and more in synch with one another. Other benefits include an increased overall positive mood while on the job and a much greater capacity to deal with the stressors inherent in the work. This is an important advancement in law enforcement, and a potent example of how gratitude, appreciation, and positive regard can transform even the most necessary and sometimes dangerous jobs.

A better mood, better performance, and an expanded capacity for managing stressful situations can be available for you too, as well as your participants. All of these are obvious benefits of the simple act of orienting toward gratitude and appreciation. In a moment that is potentially difficult, remembering our appreciation expands the field of the heart, and is as useful in fieldwork as your notebook and pen. Harken back to a moment when you have been asked to go on location, or provide contextual work through field interviews. As you drive up, you feel a nervousness tingle over your whole body. It feels risky to go to someone's home or workplace, and in truth it can be. But in this example, you have taken all safety precautions, and are just feeling the nerves of a new situation. Right here is a good time to invoke gratitude, smooth the rhythms of the heart, and get into coherence.

But this is not the end of this story. Let's look deeper into what else is occurring with and between our hearts.

Empathy in the Field of Heart Awareness

The heart generates the largest electromagnetic field in the body.[18] Using exquisitely sensitive magnetometers (called SQUID detectors), this field can be detected as radiating several feet away from a person's outer body. There is a collection of work that shows that not only is your heart "broadcasting" this field, it's receiving, interpreting, and adjusting based on others' electromagnetic signals in your proximity, engaging in a type of Bluetooth cardio-electromagnetic communication.[19]

But what exactly is being communicated? These subtle energetic indicators are intricately linked to our emotional states. If you're feeling agitated, stressed, loving, or tired, your heart is sending out the signals and others' hearts are reading them. This is where "trust your heart" originates—it knows exactly how people are feeling. It's the brain that interprets, interpolates, and fills in the gaps with story and past conditioning. The brain isn't wrong; it's just using a different dataset than the immediate information the heart is receiving and processing.

What's more, research shows that our ability to feel another through this field is variable, depending on the quality of signals being generated by our own hearts. Noisy signals (from agitation) equal noisy reception. When in coherence (appreciation), our ability to detect others' heart fields is enhanced.[20]

A part of you may be wondering if this is a good thing. What if someone is having a really sketchy day and they're sending out signals you don't want? It turns out that being coherent also makes us more internally stable and broadens our emotional container. We are less susceptible to any negative influences we may be interacting with.

Sharing of emotional states (through mirror neurons, limbic resonance, and our electromagnetic fields) is happening all around you, and within you.

By understanding that all of this is occurring, we have another rich source of primary, alive data with which to help ourselves and others intentionally create an atmosphere of enjoyable, open possibility. Giving our cognitive mind the rigor of science helps us know and be what we already and always were. Using our bodies as instruments, we can fine tune our perceptions, rely on our limbic system, our heart, and the communication between the two to guide us into more satisfying interactions with our work life.

Part I: The Ingredients of Empathic Connection

EMOTIONAL INTELLIGENCE AND EMOTIONAL AGILITY

"We think we listen, but very rarely do we listen with real understanding, true empathy. Yet listening, of this very special kind, is one of the most potent forces for change that I know."

—Carl Rogers, American psychologist

In 1995, Daniel Goleman published *Emotional Intelligence: Why It Can Matter More Than IQ*, a book introducing the world to a now-familiar concept. There are quizzes and TED talks galore about this subject, and it is widely used as a metric to determine a person's aptitude for management. In conducting qualitative research, we draw heavily from our emotional intelligence. It could even be said that this is one of the most fundamental components of what differentiates an effective researcher from one who is not. One may have all the right skills, but without keen emotional awareness and agility, much nuance can be lost.

According to Goleman, the elements that make up an emotionally intelligent person can be broken down into four categories: self-awareness, self-management, social awareness, and relationship management.

Initially, we learn about our emotional states. Next comes our ability to manage our emotional states and engender a positive outlook on them. These first two stages are self-focused, just as in our childhood development. Next, as an emotionally intelligent being, we develop the capacity to see into other people's worlds, thereby developing empathy and social awareness. It is at this stage that we develop the ability to care about the homeless population, or sense that we are negatively affecting our friends by our complaints. Finally, in the last stage, we develop relationship management skills. We become inspired to help resolve conflict within our communities, be a team player, and aspire to lead others.

We need a daily practice and a good support system to get to know our own emotional self, to turn toward difficult emotions and situations, rather than trying to overcome them. This is where emotional agility comes in. Going deeper, beyond the societies' current status quo, takes a willingness to lean into discomfort, to learn new ways that strengthen and expand our capacity to handle more difficult situations.

Later in this book, we will outline some specific tools that a Connected Researcher can employ for expanding our capacity to *stay with*—as it applies to research, difficult and pleasant emotions alike, and potent and powerful interactions, all while keeping kindness for ourselves. But for now, let's build the logic behind it and take a look at emotional agility, as outlined by Susan David, the author of *Emotional Agility*. We will look briefly at how it enables us to masterfully facilitate research sessions with an open heart and mind.

She says, "Emotional agility is a process that enables us to navigate life's twists and turns with self-acceptance, clear-sightedness, and an open mind. The process isn't about ignoring difficult emotions and thoughts. It's about holding those emotions and thoughts loosely, facing them courageously and compassionately, and then moving past them to ignite change in your life."[21]

In David's book she shares four key concepts that lead to possessing the emotional equivalent of an athletic, agile body. Paraphrased in our own words, the four keys are:

- ***Acknowledge.*** The ability to pause and admit that a difficult state is arising—rather than brushing it off or denying our feelings—is the basis for moving through difficulty to feeling more resourced.
- ***Take a step back.*** This step involves sending an invitation to the curious witnessing part of yourself, one that is slightly less overwhelmed by the current state and willing to see around the sides of it. Essentially, you learn to see yourself as the person sitting on the bank of the river, watching the water go by, rather than being carried off with the flowing current.
- ***Remember what you want.*** The Zen teacher Flint Sparks often reminds his students that "discipline is remembering what you want." Your core values and purpose keep you on track, so that you can check impulsive behaviors with your true aspiration in the world.
- ***Keep going.*** "Practice and all is coming," says Pattabhi Jois, a teacher who's among the vanguard of yogis bringing yoga to the West. Wisdom traditions tell us that each moment is about continual, small, and kind adjustments to keep us on course. By being willing to try and adjust, we are more able to make mistakes, make amends, and keep going.

When we are experiencing a strong sensation, like physical or emotional pain, we know that the impulse is to recoil, to withdraw - and for good evolutionary reasons. Instead of reflexively withdrawing from strongly felt emotions, however, we can sometimes choose to engage the body's signals in service of relying on it as a first responder to emotional information: an immediate, subconscious wealth of direction towards wisdom, wholeness, emotional intelligence, and agility.

As we learn about this skill, we can begin to practice it, to feel it. Once we start to feel things at the same time as thinking things, we begin to live like this more and more, sensing not only the thinking realms, but acknowledging the feeling ones. Then we begin to expand that sphere and remember that we can feel others. And it actually is some of the most trustworthy information that you can receive from a person, well beyond what a person is saying.

We have seen how our prefrontal cortex is working all of the time to help us with filters: the things we don't say, the impulses we don't act on. These cortical layers present our image to the world, and keep us and others safe. But underneath how our egos think we are supposed to be, our body is acting in wise ways automatically and continuously, and it is these subtle and not so subtle signals that give us clues to another person's body systems—including the nervous system.

THE BODY SPEAKS

Listening and Understanding One Another Through the Lens of the Body

Many of us have been to a yoga or meditation class where we are instructed to "listen to your body." Often in context this means not to injure or push yourself too far, which is good advice. Let's take it a step further.

Right now, where you are, without adjusting anything, take a second to check in with your body. Notice that slight pain in your right hip, or the way you are tightening your left shoulder? What do you notice, right now? Perhaps the shoulders drop as you read and acknowledge that for the sixtieth time today, you have found yourself scrunching your shoulders. Maybe you notice your breathing, where you can feel it, and where you can't. Can you feel your posture, or the places that are touching the chair or the earth? All of these subtle signals are happening continuously, all day long.

When we get curious about how we hold our left shoulder, tighter and more constricted than the other, or how we don't breathe into our full belly, we can start to see our patterns, beliefs, thoughts, the ways of being and seeing the world. Now when we recognize a slightly lifted left shoulder, we can tell we're a little nervous, and possibly feeling shy. We can check in as we sit in a research session and notice a slightly lifted left shoulder. We can savor the fact that we can see this pattern and then make a different choice. By acknowledging slight nervousness or shyness, smiling internally at it and letting it go, our energy frees up to engage in the task at hand and listen to the participant. And maybe notice that they too are holding their shoulder a little tightly, and so give them an extra smile of acceptance as well.

The Vagus Nerve

By now we are beginning to see how the brain, the heart, and the body flow together to seamlessly create our reality. Our minds are ruled by both intellect and intuition, informed by and in an intricate dance with our hearts. Information on the outside and information on the inside combine into a cohesive version of the world.

The body houses the brain and the heart, but it is not just a sack filled with blood, bacteria, and bones. Interwoven into the intricate world of perception is our nervous system. Seated deeply within the body and running the entire length of the spine is the vagus nerve. And like the mighty Ganges or Euphrates rivers that feed and nourish the entire land, our vagus nerve plays a big role in the regulation of the heart and mind. This mighty nerve controls the parasympathetic nervous system, the place of rest and digestion. It also controls the sympathetic response, our impulse to fight or flee.

Imagine King Herod's gardens, full of blossoming fruit trees, flowers of every kind, waterfalls, and birdsong. While you experience this you lay in a hammock, smack in the middle of it. This feeling of relaxed enjoyment is coming from the information in the vagus nerve, telling you that all is well and you may safely rest here in this beautiful place, a downward regulation.

Part I: The Ingredients of Empathic Connection

Now imagine that as you nap, gently moving and swaying in the balmy breeze, you suddenly hear a rustling in the bushes. At first, you pass it off as a small rodent, but then a twig breaks and something in you knows to snap to attention. The hairs on your arms raise, and your heartbeat quickens. Before the hungry tiger can pounce, you have leapt from your repose, grabbed your spear, and hurled it directly at the sneaking cat lurking in the bushes. As the monster flees, you notice your heart racing, your skin cold and clammy, and your breath now so rapid and deep that it could provide wind for a small sailboat. All of this happened before your brain ever had a chance to think "It's a tiger—run!" That is the vagus nerve, the nervous system, and the fight or flight response in action.

Fight, flight, or freeze is the nervous system's way of dealing with life-threatening stress. Cortisol is the main hormone responsible for the quick energy needed to mobilize. Cortisol is produced by the adrenal glands, which sit atop the kidneys in the back body. Think of cortisol as your body's built in alarm system.

Before the brain ever thinks or reasons about danger, our vagus nerve is in full swing, activating the sympathetic nervous system, calling for the cortisol needed to run or fight for our very lives. And it is this same cranial nerve, the vagus nerve that activates the calm, rest, and relax after the threat is gone.

In modern life, we are rarely threatened by the tiger in the woods. Our tigers have turned into road-rage filled drivers or screens filled with war games and real wars near and far. But our bodies react the same way. To our bodies, watching a gory horror film on a big screen or actually being attacked by the zombies are often perceived as the same thing. And our bodies, built with a wise and inherent system to protect themselves, produce what is needed to survive.

When a person is feeling threatened, whether from a tiger or a feeling of shame about the website they are trying to use in a sterile lab environment, the vagus nerve tells the adrenal glands to produce more cortisol, in case a quick escape is needed. The person under perceived threat is then left with a body full of hormones that will require movement to process. The metabolism of cortisol is directly related to the movement of the muscles of the body, but usually we keep still, planting a forced smile atop a worried brow and try to "just relax." We call this dysregulation. Dysregulation happens when the vagus nerve sends a signal to fight, flee, or freeze, and it is as instantaneous as a blink of an eye.

Dysregulation can happen at any moment in a research session, especially when people are asked to use a new and difficult product, or tell their story that involves trauma. As Connected Researchers we are trained to watch for and help participants remain in a window of tolerance. Think of this as a river having two banks. On one side is hyperarousal, and on the other is hypo arousal. One way is too stimulated, and the other is too relaxed, frozen, or comatose. We want to be able to help people stay in the middle.

A Connected Researcher can sense when a person is leaving their window of tolerance. It is not a likely occurrence to see many people who are completely dysregulated, to the point of actual fighting or freezing, for example. But sometimes people do feel stressed in a research session. Being prepared as a Connected Researcher gives you the skills to go into people's places of business or homes with tools for helping people stay within their window of tolerance—and helping you stay within yours. We notice if someone seems stressed, and we give them a chance to look around, reorient themselves, take a break, or find beauty. We offer humor to lighten the moment, and allow the person to relax into a very human interaction.

Remember that when our brains, hearts, and hands are in coherence, we are in our most creative place. We want our participants to be in this creative place as well, so recognizing stress at its onset can give us the information we need to slow down, take a different direction, and offer kindness, reopening the field of possibility.

A Connected Researcher is also aware of their own window of tolerance. Long-term stress from overworking shortens the window of tolerance, and so creates a stage for reactivity and burnout. A Connected Researcher knows that in order to keep that window wide, daily stress needs a place to process, metabolize, and dissolve. Physical activity, even gentle, slow exercise, is one sure way to metabolize the hormones of stress, activate the vagus nerve to calm and relax the nervous system, and flood the body with relief.

Deep breathing stimulates the vagus nerve and acts as a brake for the production of the cortisol stress hormone. Focusing on our exhalation, and in particular lengthening our exhale, tells the vagus nerve that all is well. It slows the heart rate, and returns body systems to normal functioning. Finding the right exercise and breathing activities that are replenishing is a continual proactive practice that the Connected Researcher takes time for each day.

It takes attention to live in an awakened state. We cannot prevent stress from happening, but we can imbue our lives with practices, activities, and beliefs that help keep us healthy. Seeing exercise as a way to keep mentally healthy, above the added benefit of a healthy looking body, is key to living a connected life. Connecting to yourself with a daily regimen of self-care through exercise, meditation, and alignment with purpose helps you have more room to connect with others.

Exercise: Seeing with the Eyes, Heart, Gut

This exercise is intended to illustrate the fact that we can begin to use more of our body to gather somatic data in addition to observational data during a research session. The interview questions are simple and without meaning, in order to help you take a deep dive into noticing the feedback you are getting from three key areas: your brain, your heart, and your nervous system. It is a simple yet profound way to begin to unlock the door to broader perception, using your whole body as a sensitive data collection instrument.

Pair up with someone. Decide who will be the interviewer first.

Become mindful of your body. Feel your feet, your seat, and whatever is touching the floor or the chair. Decide to listen to the subtle cues of the body for this exercise.

Eyes

As the interviewer, bring awareness into your eyes.

Find out how your participant's morning was. Watch the person, bringing special attention to what you see while you interview. Do your eyes dart around, examine, or look for changes in the person? See if you can notice the overall attitude you have while watching the person speak, with the focus originating from your eyes.

Switch as interviewer and interviewee and repeat the experiment.

Heart

1. Interviewer, bring awareness to your heart.

2. Find out what this person's weekend plans are. See them through the lens of your heart while you interview. What do you notice about this approach? Are you listening differently? Do you have a preference?

3. Switch and repeat the experiment.

Gut

1. Interviewer, bring awareness to your gut.

2. Ask about a movie or series they've just finished watching. See them through the aperture of your gut while you interview and notice what this is like. Do you have an intuitive sense of what they are talking about? What is the information you are receiving from your own gut? Do their words match what you are sensing and feeling from them?

3. Switch and repeat the experiment.

PART II
THE HEART OF UX PRINCIPLES

THE HEART OF UX PRINCIPLES

Often, we come to the field of UX research because of our basic desire to help people, to tell people's stories, and to be a part of advancing technologies that are shaping the modern world. We are told to empathize, and we are already empathic sponges, so it works well. We find a niche for our sensing and feeling hearts, and we excel at understanding what others need. But our work starts to feel lackluster in no time. Bound to the scripted repetitive interviews, the painstaking time on task demands, and one too many hundred-page reports to a team that will never read our findings, we burn out.

How do we as researchers wake up and make our lives meaningful? How do we finally, once and for all, step off the hamster wheel and walk out into the light and satisfaction of real and meaningful connection?

In the Heart of UX approach, the researcher is intricately trained in the art of seeing deeply, following curiosity, and above all else, being in a state of presence. The aim is to understand the person's experience and what is underlying their behaviors, to resonate with that experience, and to bring the underlying beliefs, thoughts, and opinions to the surface.

When we understand people more fully, we are able to deliver the most accurate account of a person's story, made more robust with the richness of true connection. Seeing underneath the layers and patterns of belief reveals and uplifts both the facilitator and the participant, revealing that each person is steeped in basic goodness. As Proust says it, "The real voyage of discovery consists not in seeking new landscapes, but in having new eyes."

The Heart of UX is grounded in basic principles. We say the principles are the foundation of our work, and we believe in them like the earth beneath our feet as we walk the path of self-discovery. As facilitators, we return to them when we are lost, or are unsure of how best to support our participants. They infuse every breath of what we do in a research session, illuminating the essential orientation and guiding our way.

PRINCIPLE ONE: POSITIVE PRESENCE

> *"The words that people say are pretty much insignificant when set next to how they are. This is important to understand if one is to catch the 'stories' of this human race."*
>
> —Nic Askew, Soul Biographies®

It is often said in the Hakomi Method that "the state of the facilitator is the most important thing." We facilitate consciousness—that is to say, we lead people into a place that is reflective and curious, open and compassionate. But how is this achieved? By assuming a state of positive presence, or natural presence. And as we've seen, one limbic system stabilized on mutual care and full attention brings coherence between both. Another person can literally borrow our state of acceptance and kindness, then bring it to themselves and the world outside of them.

Presence to the Rescue

Have you ever been in an emergency, then watched a capable and strong EMT come into the room, and everything returns to normal? As a mother, I sure have. One night, after many days of a terrible flu virus, our daughter began feeling weak and pale. She looked like she was dying. As I helped her out of the bathroom, she lost consciousness and fell into my arms. We called 911, and help rushed in minutes later. As the firefighters circled her limp body and plugged in diagnostics, she came to. Her pulse calmed and her color returned. By the time they carried her to the couch, she was smiling and joking with them.

They knew that she was not dying but had passed out from dehydration. Their quick action and steady attitude revived her faster than any drug could. They joked and gently explained what happened. The pounding in my ears slowed, and we returned to normal. How did this happen? The EMTs were confident and caring, and their nervous systems were stable and calm. And that calmed and stabilized us. The EMTs arrived with a positive presence, and helped us connect to the overall health of our daughter, rather than our fear and distress.—Jessica

---

Presence has a subtle, felt quality to it. When we can be immediate, current, and focused in the now, when we bring our presence to any situation, others respond in kind. This applies to research, as well as all areas of our lives. As research moderators, we bring our full selves to the scene of any interview. We listen attentively, and with the skills outlined below, we make sure that our participant feels seen, heard, and understood. And this all happens through the gateway of presence.

How do we approach embodying a positive presence? There are reliable techniques, one of them being to actively assume the attitude, the orientation that each person is an inspiration. Even if our conscious mind can't see it in someone in the moment, we can choose to trust that the inspiration is there if only we choose to find it. In this way, our intention to do so paves the way to the possibility.

The ROI of Presence

Within the first ten minutes of our research session together, I could see Jeff exhibit a countenance of disinterest and incredulity. He doodled on his paper while I took a moment to ready the next task. There was a war raging inside of him, but on the outside it would appear as boredom. Relying on my knowledge that limbic systems co-regulate, I could feel the agitation deep within his body. It felt to me like an uncomfortable nervousness, a quivering beneath the surface of my own skin.

I noticed my own sensation, took a guess and delivered a simple statement to him as an attempt to connect on a deeper level. I softened my eyes, then remembered that this person was an inspiration. This simple remembrance gave me the courage to name the internal bind that I thought he was in.

"You're in a bind, huh?"

"I'm just really worried," he said. "I carry all of the burden of the whole team and answer to my director for meeting our quarterly goals. We're so far behind. I can't spend any more time on this, and yet I don't know how to move forward. I don't know what to do next."

I wasn't attached to whether my guess was right. In fact, making a mistaken guess can reveal data that is just as useful. But in this case, I felt the discomfort, named it as a bind, and opened the door for Jeff to tell me a deeper issue that he was working with, below the surface of our interview. This opening was as simple as naming my guess about his situation.

As his fear and emotions poured out, it became clear that the product we were there to test was not going to help his stress; in fact, it was making it worse. He had been forced to use an internal product that made his work more difficult than it had to be. This fact was new information to the developers and management, who were proceeding in good faith on a path that in actuality wasn't helpful. This led to more straightforward and honest discussions between teams, and they were able to course-correct.

I could have easily been put off at Jeff's doodling, and assumed he was disengaged and not worth my time. He certainly didn't seem to value my time. But by relying instead on positive presence, I deepened the connection and trusted that the way of being with this person was more important than the idea of getting the tasks accomplished. This simple act was part of saving a Fortune 100 company tons of money. It enabled them to create a more meaningful, useful tool.—Jessica

---

We hear designers, product owners, managers, and executives alike all sharing similar stories. As researchers, we are usually brought into situations like these in order to bring some empirical evidence to design challenges, and provide some answers. We know that what people say and do are the primary data sources to provide this evidence. What we are proposing is that we should rely on our own minds and bodies as a primary data source as well.

Bringing our full presence and attention, we connect to our own body systems, trusting that they are also registering sensations of other body systems around us. Then, inviting an attitude of experimentation, we take a guess at what the other might be feeling at a deeper level, and speak directly to that place. Our attention and orientation can be thought of as that of a caring and kind grandmother or grandfather: open, non-judgmental, fully and completely present. We drop the agenda and orient around getting into coherence with that person. We see them as a whole and capable being, no matter what they are expressing in the moment. We remember their basic goodness, and ours as well. Doing so elicits an authentic meeting, a more vulnerable exchange and a caring outcome. Oh, and rich research data!

In addition to being non-judgmental, positive presence has, of course, positivity at its core. "Positive questions lead to positive change," says David Cooperrider, the pioneer of Appreciative Inquiry, a system we'll go into more deeply later. Change, on a small or large scale, requires great momentum which must be fueled by clean burning, powerful energy. This energy comes from grounding ourselves in a positive core. When we are frustrated, anxious, stressed and unhappy, our awareness narrows and we can't take in what's available around us.

Note your physical expressions the next time you feel this way. You'll see that your gaze is down; your voice is more flat and monotone. It's like driving around at night without your lights, relying on the dim, ambient glare to get around. Positive energy, however, is more like driving in full daylight, with your brain taking in a full host of high definition information. Eye tracking studies bear this out. They show that when we are primed for a positive mindset, our eyes move around much more and are taking in more of our surroundings, seeing the psychological embodied in the physical.

This is not only important to remember for ourselves as moderators. We also would prefer that our participants are in a positive field. We want them to be able to express themselves fully, see opportunities and possibilities in their own lives so that we may be more likely to co-create amazing products and solutions worthy of our life's energy. So, how do we also elicit a positive mindset from our participants during a research session? Your positive presence helps a great deal, and a complementary technique is called positive framing. This involves reframing from a negative statement or belief to instead point at the positive desire. This is a skill and takes practice, as we shall see.

"Happiness does not depend on what you have or who you are," said the Buddha, "It solely relies on what you think."

Something Out of Nothing

As the morning bustle settled, I looked around the kitchen for the next thing on my to-do list before heading out to work. "The chicken," I remembered and exclaimed under my breath. Taking the raw chicken from its wrapper, I placed it in the crock pot, ready to create a delicious green enchilada chicken stew that would bubble and aromatically fill the house all day. At the end of a long day away, coming home to a hot dinner is one of my favorite ways to nourish myself and others.

Just then, terror struck. No enchilada sauce! The whole recipe depended on that ingredient, and I didn't have time to go to the store. I thought for a moment and then noticed the place of lack that had been triggered inside of me. I reframed the question. "What do I have to combine with the chicken?" I found a can of tomatoes in the very bare pantry. "Hmmm, this might help." Then I remembered the herbs I had growing in the garden. I hurried outside with a smile to collect freshly grown basil, oregano, and parsley. It was not at all what I had planned or expected, but dinner turned out to be delicious and fresh, beyond what I imagined.—Jessica

Exercise: Something Out of Nothing to Reframe Your Life

*"Reframing: To take an issue or problem or gap—what we want **less** of—and re-frame it into a positive topic—what we want **more** of."*

—Center for Appreciative Inquiry

This example of inner resourcing, mindfulness, and reframing is simple, and we are given these types of opportunities all day every day. Our lives are filled with chances to pause, become aware of the prevailing thought pattern, and choose again. Often, these small but continual choices go undiscovered as gateways to presence, opportunities to see the strength in the moment. But as we begin practicing positive framing, we jump the gap to become more aware of possibilities around us—and that awareness is power. Emboldened by the power of choosing our own perspective, we can claim and reframe our attitude.

Here's how reframing works, as taught by the Appreciative Inquiry method:

1. **Name it**: What is the problem, the issue, or the thing you don't want?

2. **Flip it**: What is the positive opposite? The thing you do want?

3. **Frame it**: What is the desired outcome if this positive thing is true?

Try this technique out the next time you hear someone, even yourself, speaking from a negative, deficit-seeking place. Notice the effects on the body, your energy, their energy, and what may now be possible to achieve what it is desired.

Try it in your daily life. The next time you notice a negative belief, pause. Give yourself a few moments to take a deep breath and ask yourself "what could be possible here?" Make a choice to reframe the problem into an opportunity.

PRINCIPLE TWO: MINDFULNESS

To be a highly functioning researcher, you often must juggle many things all at once. Multiple projects with competing timelines, stakeholders from across business units with different requests and expectations, all of this and more. Mindfulness is a practice that will sustain you, your life, your health, your energy, and your potency over time in your work. Every deepening in the Heart of UX depends on it. It can be described as an active, cultivated awareness. Without it, we are in a state of ordinary consciousness: waking, surface-level awareness.

Ordinary consciousness is of course very useful, and we're not suggesting to do away with it, as it provides a baseline for us to do so many of the things we need to do as living beings. When we are in mindfulness, however, our experience and our awareness expands—we are attuned to the signals of our bodies, the subtle whispers of sounds around us. The light breeze across our face from the air conditioner that we hadn't noticed before. The slight aching in the left quadriceps from sitting long hours on the flight. It's a subtle tuning into the inner landscape, while maintaining awareness with what is occurring outside. It begins with a willingness to pay attention, to suspend judgment or reactivity, and to simply observe.

An Introduction to Mindfulness

> *"If you sprinkle one ounce of vinegar over two hundred tons of sugar, no one will ever taste the vinegar."*
>
> —*Rumi*

There is an old adage that describes mindfulness and likens it to a teaspoon of salt being placed in a vessel of water. If your vessel is quite small, say the size of an espresso cup, a teaspoon of salt may cause the water to taste so salty that a person could not comfortably drink it. However, you pour that same teaspoon of salt into a five gallon jug of water, and the salt is hardly perceptible. This is the action of mindfulness. Over time, sitting still and becoming aware of one's experience, both inside and out, we develop a greater capacity—we enlarge the container of awareness (the jug), becoming capable of experiencing the salt in our lives amidst a broader and wider field of contentment. The salt is the same, sodium chloride, and the water is the same, H_2O, but our experience of the salt is different with a bigger container. This is one of the benefits of establishing a mindfulness practice.

Being mindful is not the same thing as being relaxed or chilled out. In fact it is being ultra-aware, and specifically attentive. It does seem to have a side effect though, and that is contentment. Santosha is a Sanskrit word that loosely is translated as contentment. However, this contentment is not complacency. We do not sit idly back and remove all feelings, becoming an aloof automaton. Instead we broaden our awareness, and our ability, to feel more, to allow more, to appreciate what we already and always are. Like feeding a starving child, we begin, little by little, offering only a drop or two of gratitude, a small morsel of food for our starving souls. Awareness broadens our experience, and helps us see beyond the faces and voices of fear, anger, in our minds—to the open and spacious reality around us. It also helps us become familiar with patterns and ways that we hold ourselves back. When we become familiar with these habits that are not serving us, we can recognize them sooner, and choose again. It is in this remembering, and returning that our lives are brought back to the underlying beauty, contentment and available joy that abounds in each moment.

If you're reading this in a fairly quiet space, you can tap into this right now while you read. Slow down, just a little. Turn on your inner awareness. Feel the air on your skin. Listen to the sounds around you, letting them wash over you like waves. Note the smell and temperature of the room. Feel what is happening in your body. Notice something you hadn't been aware of before this paragraph began. This is the basic experience of mindfulness.

We strongly encourage taking up a regular meditation practice in order to support a feeling of spaciousness in your heart and mind. This comes from sitting quietly on a regular basis—and it doesn't need to be an elaborate or time-consuming addition to your already full day. Studies conducted by Amishi P. Jha (professor of psychology and director of contemplative neuroscience at the University of Miami) show that sitting for as little as twelve minutes a day activates a cascade of brain chemicals and neuronal processes that elicit a sustained state of calm and wellbeing.[22] There's no need to do anything special, other than sit very still in a quiet room, pay attention to your breath, and cultivate a curiosity as to what arises.

One way mindfulness enhances our experience is by increasing neural integration in the brain, facilitating more coordination and balance, problem solving, and self-regulation abilities.[23] This integration also connects the brain and the nervous system more succinctly for optimal functioning and communication between the two.

It's not just the brain that benefits from mindfulness. Research reveals that our immune systems are improved, genetic regulation occurs which prevents inflammation and keeps your cells youthful, and cardiovascular benefits abound including lowered blood pressure.[24] It turns out that our whole body, and many ailments of a modern stressed life can be managed with a regular mindfulness practice. Taking up a practice of mindfulness helps us stay healthy, youthful, and in optimal health. It also increases our capacity for being aware, and once we are aware we can act with greater wisdom, and mindful care.

A Connected Researcher utilizes mindfulness as a way to pay attention to their own bodies as well as to what is happening in the research sessions and the broader project arena. It allows you to become familiar with and trust your intuition. This means you remain in a state of inquiry rather than surety. There is a saying in the Zen tradition, "Not knowing is most intimate." Allow yourself to be unsure, to be adjustable, and to follow what you become aware of, in yourself and the world around you.

In his book *Aware*, Dan Siegel gives a very practical model to help us visualize mindfulness with a tool he calls "The Wheel of Awareness."[25] Imagine a wagon wheel, or a bicycle wheel, with the center (hub), and an outer rim. In this model, the hub at the center is basic Awareness, the hub of "knowing." As you move around the rim, we see all of the "knowns of life:" our five senses, mental activities, bodily sensations, and connections. From Awareness at the center, we imagine a singular spoke, which is our attention. Where we place our attention is where our awareness goes. We can move the spoke of attention around the outer rim, surveying and exploring the input from our senses, our sensations and other sensory input. Dan tells us that "by distinguishing the wide array of knowns on the rim from each other and from the knowing of awareness in the hub itself, we can differentiate the components of consciousness." This mental model is one that can be very helpful as we begin to explore mindfulness as a tool to deepen our abilities as researchers. Getting to know how we see ourselves and others gives us insight into the ways in which we organize our experiences, and with that kind of big picture view, much more of the landscape can be seen. It also trains our minds to remember how powerful our attention is. Flint Sparks says, "what you practice is what grows." Where we place our attention is a choice, and this is a powerful thing indeed.

Before your next research project begins, make an intention to establish a personal mindfulness practice. This is the only way to even begin to tell if you are getting out of your window of tolerance with your workload. If you're not aware of the individual, subtle signals your body is sending you when you're reaching your capacity edge, you won't be able to make minor course corrections and it will be a lot harder to recover.

A personal mindfulness practice can take a myriad of forms. Some of them may seem obvious: meditation, yoga, chanting, breathing techniques—these are all classic practices that get you in touch with your body, mind, awareness, and heart.

But there are many other forms of mindfulness practices that exist: gardening, cycling, sewing, cooking—any activity that aligns your body and mind in such a way that it allows you to self-study, while also maintaining awareness of what is around you. It eventually brings you to a place where you are observing your experience instead of just being immersed in it. It can be likened to the difference between being immersed in the flow of the stream, versus being an active observer, perched on the bank, watching as the stream goes by.

Easy Mindfulness You Can Do Anywhere

Due to the pace we're all familiar with, it's not always possible to even take five minutes in a quiet place to re-center. Here's a simple three-step practice that will help you ground into your own experience right now, no matter what is going on:

1. Establish yourself in your body. Feel where your feet connect to the floor. If sitting, also feel the support of the chair beneath and behind you.

2. Place your attention on your breath and follow your breathing. No need to force anything to change, just follow it as it is.

3. Notice something that you hadn't noticed before. Expand this noticing to other aspects of your awareness, in this moment.

If your mind wanders (and it will), just note or name that too as it happens, maybe even internally saying something like "oh, planning ahead thoughts…" It doesn't matter, just gently bring your awareness back to your breath in this moment and keep going for as long as it feels interesting.

> You can employ this simple practice in a meeting, in an elevator, or at a stoplight. Over time, you can even do this in the middle of a conversation if you feel yourself drifting off or caught by a big emotion. It brings you back to yourself by reliably connecting you to your own source and the resourcing that is always available.

PRINCIPLE THREE: CONGRUENCE

Congruence is the quality of agreement, forming a harmonious whole. A Connected Researcher relies on a basic belief in wholeness and understands that there is a basic underlying wisdom at work. They embrace a Gestalt viewpoint, one where the whole is greater than the sum of its parts. There is a trust that bringing all of the parts together stimulates creativity, whether in a group or within one's own being. There is also an acceptance of all of the parts, not only outside in other people, but within ourselves. We seek union between the mind and body, a union between the parts of ourselves that we like and don't like. Mind-body cohesion is a tall order, but one we are definitely ready for as a species.

Descartes famously popularized the "mind-body problem" in his *Discourse on the Method*, in which he asserts that he can doubt that he has a body, but cannot doubt that he has a mind, and therefore sees the mind and the body as two very separate things. Through the lens of separation, and dissection of parts, incredible technologies like calculus and Cartesian geometry were created. Although we as a species often need to dissect concepts to further our understanding of the greater whole, we know through advances in modern quantum physics—and some ancient spiritual teachings—that we keep coming around to a more nondual realization: all seemingly separate things are actually part of the whole. This leaves nothing out, including you.

Removing artificial separations is a driving force of this work, and an underlying reason we believe that many of us got into this field in the first place. We are seeking to bring our users' desires, unmet needs, and workflows into the forefront of conversations with those who develop and ship products. This is about connection, and it's difficult to have connection when the needs of users are incongruent with what is being developed.

We propose that in order to exhibit congruence in our work and our daily lives, we must also apply this aim to our internal landscapes. In an industry that often demands a high bar of performance and deliverables, we are very likely to encounter the inner critic. This inner critic is a voice most of us are all too familiar with. When we make a mistake, for example, it's often followed by a voice that is quite rough. It takes a variety of forms, but often the mark of the critic is one of demeaning or dismissive language. "Just get it together, why don't you," you might say to yourself, or a sarcastic "Way to go, meathead!" Already you can probably hear the familiar flavor of your own inner critic. We UXers are often people with drive, and with drive comes as a spoken or unspoken expectation of perfection.

It turns out that we can't exile the critic within us to a distant place where we can no longer hear them. Instead, seemingly paradoxically, a radical shift happens when we turn to meet the critic, and accept them as a misguided protector. This part of your personality can be seen as something inside of you that is actually trying to make sure that you are loved, valued, and accepted. It rains down insults in order to protect the more vulnerable parts of you. For example, the part of you that is so tired it wants to give up. Or the part of you that is still grieving the loss of your dog. Our inner critics want to keep us productive, and useful to society. While this is a good cause, it is a misguided method.

We have a chance to practice bringing these two parts into congruence: the critical part and the part being criticized. We can invite both of the parts to the dinner table for a discussion. When we do this, we invite a conversation that can be potent and release hidden stores of energy and vitality. For example, when we allow the tired and discouraged parts to have some space inside our vast and spacious heart right alongside our inner critic, these parts no longer operate under the surface—and there is opportunity for congruence.

Why are we presenting a discussion on working with the different parts of our internal landscapes? Because a large part of our jobs involves moderating discussions between many different people, departments, business units, and companies. If our differences inside are not seen and allowed, we will continue to over-exert in working with the parts on the outside. There is a saying: "As above, so below." We can extend this to say "as within, so without."

Awareness of the conversations between the different aspects of our personality has an interesting effect of being able to choose where to operate from. In other words, being aware gives us choice. Choice gives us the possibility of inviting what is aligned, connected, and whole, congruent. We can get all parts of us on board, in the same conversation, and working for the same goal. This frees all of that energy we were using to fight with ourselves to now work in a cohesive, aligned way.

That is how we can get the five research sessions done today and not feel so exhausted and burned out that we snap at our loved ones when we come home. Suddenly, our energy is a little more focused, clear, alive, and abundant. Our work turns from seeing all of the problems to trying to fix them, moving to facilitate wholeness, internal agreement, and compassion. This, in turn, makes us more available to others, more empathic, and it enhances our ability to connect with our participants and hear their truest, deepest needs. After all, we are here to serve humanity through directing the forms of technology, right?

If this whole idea seems daunting, we offer the exercise below, developed by the renowned psychologist Tara Brach to help facilitate a meaningful conversation with your inner critic.[26] The next time you feel yourself at war within, take some time in a place where you feel safe, comfortable, and relaxed and walk through the steps below. You may wish to do this at home the first time or two, as inner exploration and dialogue often requires adequate rest, recovery, and spaciousness.

Exercise: RAIN Meditation for the Inner Critic

Rain is an acronym that stands for:

Recognize
Allow
Investigate
Nurture

This exercise works by bringing mindfulness and compassion together to apply to an area of difficulty in your life, or specifically to an inner critic.

Begin by bringing your attention to the breath, and sense the possibility of relaxing along with the breath. Feel the inhalation, and invite a sense of filling up, enjoying the life energy that comes with taking the breath in. On the exhale, feel the letting go that naturally and organically wants to happen in the body.

Letting go in the shoulders
Softening the hands
Relaxing the belly
Relaxing the heart
Continuing to relax with the movement of the breath
Relax into open spaciousness

From a place of wakeful and kind curiosity, begin to scan your mind and body for any places of discomfort.

It may feel like hurt, or fear, shame, or sadness. Maybe it's a situation that comes to mind with another person. Pick something that feels like a charged reaction, but not overwhelming. Notice the details: was there a conversation? A feeling? A look? Freeze the frame of your life on this feeling in order to study it. Get to know it more deeply.

Now, begin with the R, **Recognize**.

What is the most predominant feeling? Anger, hurt, anxiety? Notice whatever internal voice might be the speaker of that overarching emotion. Name to yourself whatever it is that you are most aware of. Is there a sentence or a tone that is coming from a critical place from within you toward yourself?

Allow—Let it be there right now.

Pause. Make space for whatever is here, trusting that what is arising is the path. Allow doesn't mean you like it, or condone it or encourage the criticism. Don't go in to the criticism, instead just get curious about its language, its tone, and its particular feel. Just deepen your attention, like you are having an important conversation with a loved one.

Investigate—What wants your attention most?

What's the most difficult part of this? With Investigate, you are feeling into your body. Ask yourself, "What am I hearing, seeing, or believing when this is happening? Is the critic inside telling me that I am a failure? Or saying harsh words?" Can you begin to ask it to tell you more? Notice your body, and the sensations in the body as you begin the conversation with this inner critic.

Pay attention to your heart space; is it constricted or spacious? What is happening in your throat? Do you notice anything in your belly? Is there a constriction or maybe an ache?

What emotion might be there, mixing right in with something you are believing from this inner critic? Is there a place that feels most vulnerable in your body?

Nurture—Let energy flow.

If that vulnerable place could communicate, what would it want you to know? To investigate begins to move toward nurturing when you ask that vulnerable place, "How do you want me to be with you?"

What does it most need right now? Invite the most loving and wise part of yourself now to enter your awareness. It may help here to imagine a religious figure, teacher, or guide that embodies loving compassion for you.

Stay in contact with the vulnerability, and also notice the place in you that is unconditionally loving and wise.

Sense that you can offer what is most needed to this critical and suffering place in you. You might sense where this vulnerable place lives in your body and bring your hand to that place, offering it a tender touch.

Let energy flow from your hand into that tender place. In your own words, hear the thing that this vulnerable place most needs right now. It might be, "You are safe" or "I'm not leaving" or "I am here with you." Take your time, feeling yourself be both the beloved and the loved one, the one offering and the one receiving.

After the RAIN exercise, take some time to rest, relax, and keep letting this love in. Be aware of the quality of presence that is here. What's the sense of your own being, of who you are right now?

How has this shifted from when you began the meditation? Can you welcome this conversation between the critic and the wisdom in you to happen again? Come back, take your time, and when you are finished, return to your day.

PRINCIPLE FOUR: FOLLOW ALIVENESS

What is aliveness? It's the organic, free flowing fundamental stuff of life, the yearning, the longing toward becoming. This is the basis for creativity and it's exactly what is stirring within us as well. If we can tune into this aliveness and learn to trust and follow it, it will lead us to places we never expected to go to, stories we didn't expect to hear, and new questions that we as researchers never before thought to ask.

Aliveness and synchronicity are inexplicably linked, and the more you pay attention, the more synchronicities abound. Just like when you are thinking of your dear friend that you haven't spoken to in a while and they call you on the phone. "Meaningful coincidences," as Carl Jung described them, are synchronicities that can be seen in the world all around us. When we allow ourselves to believe in an organically moving, synchronistic universe, we begin to see a broader picture, a wider view. We begin to trust what is happening, even if we don't know why or what is happening. Some religions call it faith, which we define as the power to see past egoic grasping to something bigger, the mystery. Being okay with the mystery and not imposing a rigid idea of things, we loosen our grip and experience life and others in it as a part of a greater whole.

For a Connected Researcher, trusting the aliveness means being willing to turn on a dime. When, a few participants into your research study, you realize that the original primary research question was not actually the right question, or that it was not fully defined or understood until now, you take a step backwards. You ask the question in a new way, or take a new direction, and try again.

Often the result is an improved and engaging experience. This is the same attitude behind the RITE (Rapid Iterative Testing and Evaluation) method, and Lean UX. Both of these are methods built on a platform of progressive discovery and evolutionary change—the idea being that we are learning more about a design as we put it in front of more people—and there is an implicit flexibility to the design which evolves as the study progresses. This philosophy very much aligns with the willingness to follow aliveness.

This also has broader implications. When you follow what is alive, inside yourself as well as occurring with the participant, the session content is juicer, more robust, interesting, and therefore much more trustworthy to all who are observing it. We will break down the specific skills to illuminate this principle in the next section on techniques, but for now, understand that this is as easy as trusting what feels interesting and important to you. There is a cautionary note that's needed here which is to say that this takes practice to know when to jump off script and pivot the direction of the questions—and that is not the same thing as moving on because we feel bored.

If we are bound by lengthy scripts and focused on completing tasks, however, we can often miss what is most relevant for a person, and instead record "fake data." Fake data flows forth from a forced, unnatural scenario. Keeping tasks light and allowing organic movement through a design may elicit data and findings you could not have planned for.

I was hired to conduct an out-of-box evaluation (OOBE) on a home automation product and the sessions weren't going so well. As Participant 4 tried to use the provided directions to install the system to no avail (as with the previous sessions), her frustrations grew, with some tears even. Puzzled, defeated faces were seen around the client observation room.

Participant 5, however did something off script. He decided to take out his phone, and look to YouTube for a video on installation of a similar product.

I had a choice at this moment to redirect the person back to the current, designed experience and record a "fail" for a fourth time, to simply proceed as planned and bolster the growing dataset of evidence, or let the man watch the video and see what happened.

In a moment of insight and curiosity, I allowed him to continue. He watched the video, paused on the relevant bits as needed and as a result, the installation was completed easily. We tried the same video for subsequent sessions and, most of the remaining participants were able to complete the installation successfully. From that one session, and an intuition to let the participant follow their impulse, the team learned that adding a short instructional video to the installation flow was the best way to ensure a successful installation.—Jon-Eric

---

This is one among many examples of following what is alive. The researcher felt in his own body that something new and different was happening, and followed it. He knew, based on three prior sessions that the person would likely fail again if they were disallowed from using the video. But it wasn't just a cognitive knowing—he could feel in his own body that watching the same thing again wouldn't be interesting or enlivening. But the curiosity of "what would happen if," along with the energy present for the participants' boldness to just take out his phone without being prompted to do so, felt energizing and alive. This person was doing something real, something authentic, and there's nothing more alive than that.

For subsequent sessions, participants were invited to watch the video, and in a complete turn of events, everyone succeeded with ease and the design solution was discovered. The decision to trust what was alive led directly to the solution the product team needed.

PRINCIPLE FIVE: SYNCHRONISM

In his book *Synchronicity: An Acausal Connecting Principle*, Carl Jung wrote, "It is impossible [to explain] meaningful coincidence … therefore it cannot be a question of cause and effect, but of a falling together in time, a kind of simultaneity." In the Heart of UX, the principle of synchronism rests on the widely accepted fact that our universe is not deterministic but instead is a participatory universe, ebullient with possibility.

Arising from the science of quantum physics, the idea of a participatory universe was masterfully demonstrated by the famous delayed choice experiments pioneered by the American theoretical physicist John Wheeler. We won't go into all of the details here, but in essence, the setup goes like this. In the laboratory, light is found to behave just as a wave, not unlike waves of water or sound as it travels through a medium. Oddly, when a detector is put into place so that we can see what's happening while the light travels, the light decides to now act as a single photon, not a wave. The act of measurement reliably changes the outcome. This experiment has been repeated thousands of times since the early 1900's and points to the observer effect, as we will discuss later.

Wheeler's experiments take this even further with his delayed choice experiment. This attempted to get around the observer effect and "look under the hood" of what was happening and how the light knew it was being observed by measurements at different times in the past and future, before or after the light "knew" it was being observed. Ultimately, it has offered increasingly sophisticated evidence that light exists as both a particle and a wave, in a state of apparent simultaneity, in a state of synchronism—and that no matter when we try to observe it, the act of observation changes what is.

Because it exists in the same participatory universe as everything else, this is also necessarily true in UX research. It also points to why the authors of this book are inherently cautious of using surveys and non-moderated data collection tools as primary research instruments. When we define the questions a priori and rely on the answers that are returned, we greatly limit the field of possibility.

Our measurement reduces "what is" to a fixed idea. As Picasso famously stated, "Computers are useless, they can only provide answers." We instead are proposing that the human body-heart-mind is the most sophisticated data collection system that exists. There is a need to re-think our classical approach to research, whereby the phenomena are "out there" and we are "here" to measure and collect. We are a part of the same scene as our participants and our experiments.

Another way to refer to this is interdependent co-arising. Interdependent: we're all connected. Co-arising: we're all happening all at once. When we begin to actively see the world as an interdependent co-arising phenomenon, we find that we can no longer separate ourselves as easily as before. We can no longer see the other person as completely "other." In a participatory universe, we are all participating, simultaneously co-creating all that is arising and passing away. We have full permission to participate fully, as well as acknowledge that we are all doing so. We've seen that this invites a vulnerability and co-owning of the field that has been created between ourselves and our research participants. We will see this principle underlies much of the techniques put forth in this book.

> *"Creative energy is innate and spontaneously present. It is unborn, with no center or boundary, yet nothing exists outside of it."*
>
> —Dzigar Kongtrul

PRINCIPLE SIX: RESOURCING

If you've worked as a researcher for any length of time, you know that the work can be quite taxing at times. The pace of it can get grueling, both for ourselves and sometimes for our participants and stakeholders as well. We can get caught up in over-scoping and over-promising and then before you know it, we've exceeded our capacity to stay present and focused on what's happening. Next thing you know, the coffee's no longer working and you're nodding off while the final lab participant of the day is thinking out loud and it all sounds like a mush of buttons, and email confirmations and—what did they say?

We've all been there. This occurs as a result of a lack of personal resources, most notably time, energy, and rest. If we're way out of our zone of resourcing, we're not able to access our full capacities. Resources are our fuel, and without them, we're running on fumes and tapping into our reserves. Doing so is not only detrimental to the integrity of the data collection, but to our bodies, our health, and our well-being as well. We got into this work to make things better for all of us, ourselves included, so why leave ourselves out of needing to thrive?

What can we do? Ideally, we don't set ourselves up with such a hectic pace, but this is not always possible—and besides, we all have different tolerances for what is possible or not. Outlined in the next section are specific techniques that the

Connected Researcher uses for staying resourced, even in the face of a heroic schedule.

These six basic principles of the Heart of UX are the foundations, philosophies, and ideas that this teaching is based on. The first five: embodying a positive presence, inviting mindfulness, enjoying coherence, following aliveness, and noticing the synchronism in all things will provide the orientation from which we stand, the lens with which we see.

To fully understand resourcing as a Heart of UX principle, you need to experience it personally, in an embodied way: in your own body. In the next section, we will give you very specific techniques for practicing the principles. Think of these techniques as the principles in action. The practices will bring an embodied understanding of resourcing, plus give you ways to gain access to resources when you notice yourself becoming stressed. The resources may have been previously untapped, or unknown. The key concept is to pay care-filled attention to your own emotional state—and know that there are easy ways to reconnect when you feel adrift and empty.

Self-Compassion

It is worth stating in a UX book why we offer our words about self-compassion, and later, talk about the relief of suffering. First, not everyone gives that much thought about other people's well-being. We certainly do, and believe you do as well, because you're reading this book—and a Connected Researcher absolutely cares about people. We believe the needs of, and care for people are both at the forefront of developing and propagating technology. We're not going to be neutral in this position. Technology can be good or bad, harmful or helpful, and it's up to us as UX professionals to ensure technology lands closer to the helpful side of the spectrum as is possible. In order to do this, we must start in the place where we have the most influence and chances to practice compassion: within our own selves. Compassion for yourself extends outwards toward those around you. It cannot be done any other way.

So we have a wish for you. If there is only one thing you remember and take away from this book, may it be self-compassion. It's more complex than it may seem as an idea, and even more intricate as a practice. It involves more than eating an extra scoop of ice cream, or brushing off guilt for making a snarky comment. Self-compassion is the act of treating oneself like one's own good friend.

Offering compassion to others involves a belief that the suffering of others exists. The Latin root of the word compassion literally means "to suffer with." Imagine seeing a mother struggling across a busy intersection, holding all of the baby gear and pushing a stroller while the young child screams and thrashes to get out of her arms. Your compassionate instinct would kick in, and you'd walk over to see if you could help, or at least send her a smile. This is the same attitude that we hope to offer to ourselves.

In order to take up the practice of self-compassion, we must see all the places where we actually are not being compassionate to ourselves. At first, this can be daunting. We remember those days when we first began turning toward ourselves in this way. Jessica said, "It felt like I turned on a flashlight and a bunch of cockroaches went scattering. I was shocked and horrified to see the ways I talked to myself internally." The more we paid attention, the more the talk was everywhere, and we had to come to terms with an embedded pattern. In the Zen community, this is referenced as "ancient, tangled karma." Often these critics are inherited from our parents, grandparents, and teachers.

More advanced lessons are all around us. Author and researcher Dr. Kristin Neff from the University of Texas at Austin identifies three elements to self-compassion: self-kindness vs. self judgement, common humanity vs. isolation, and mindfulness vs. overidentification.[19]

Self-kindness says that rather than ignoring our pain or berating ourselves through self-judgment when we suffer, fail or feel inadequate, we can offer ourselves a basic kindness. We can see ourselves as human, fallible, and worthy of forgiveness. People who are kind to themselves develop a greater capacity for making mistakes.

The second element as outlined by Neff, common humanity vs. isolation, is the practice of realizing our perspective around thinking that the way that we are suffering is completely unique and personal. There is an underlying belief that says, "I am the only person making these mistakes." When we accept that we are part of a world where suffering exists, where people feel inadequate regularly, we accept ourselves as a part of this complicated and vulnerable world. Part of being alive and in a body means being imperfect, and this is something we all share.

The third and final element to Neff's self-compassion, mindfulness vs. overidentification, is precisely aligned with the Heart of UX principle of mindfulness. In mindfulness, we can learn to take a measured approach to our negative emotions and not feel as overwhelmed by them as before. We are more able to dis-identify with negative thoughts, while not suppressing or seeking escape from them. Mindfulness is walking a path between the ditches of disembodied, dispassionate aloofness and wallowing in negative beliefs and emotions about ourselves.

The Four Noble Truths of Technology

This field of User Experience emerged from the recognition that technology is being developed rapidly, and that we need to couple this growth with an understanding of its influence on the human experience to make it all work well (and work out well for us). We recognized that the adoption of new technology can be fraught with confusion, excitement, shame, alienation, joy, connection, and all of the things that we as humans bring to all things we do.

As Connected Researchers, this takes empathy to a whole new level. We recognize that suffering exists in humanity as it does in technology. We see that using technology has its dark sides, and we endeavor to keep aiming it in the service of humanity. We endeavor especially to not make things worse. Refraining from caustic opinions and an evaluative mindset allows a Connected Researcher to truly see and hear the needs of the clients, as well as the participants. Jessica says that the moment she realized she had the chance to meet many people fully during each day, to hear their story and see them as an inspiring life force, her heart opened to the realization: "I am in a unique position as a researcher to spread joy to many."

One of the primary philosophical frameworks for understanding and working with suffering and compassion are the thousands-year-old teachings of the Buddha. We're presenting some of them here as a useful framework (not as a suggested spiritual path) as many of our principles, such as mindfulness, have emerged from these teachings.

The essential teaching of the Buddha is that of the Four Noble Truths. There are many translations to these four basic statements, but the fundamentals of the meaning surrounds both the causes of and relief from suffering. It's best summed up in *The Four Noble Truths*, as summarized by the author Joko Beck.

1. Caught in the self-centered dream, only suffering;
2. Holding to self-centered thoughts, exactly the dream.
3. Each moment, life as it is, the only teacher;
4. Being just this moment, compassion's way.

The Rift, or Suffering

Now let's take a deep dive into suffering. We invite you to walk with us as we tell you a story of the Buddha, and eventually bring it all back around to research. The Buddha initially practiced an extreme version of asceticism, owning nothing and barely eating. He sat, practiced the most difficult postures, torturing and starving his body. None of this brought him to the enlightenment he was seeking. Just as he was near starvation and death, a woman came to him with a bowl of rice and milk.

From this simple offering, he had the strength to enter the forest and sit under the bodhi tree, determined to understand the source of suffering and the path from it. It is here he met self-doubt in the darkness of the night, classically embodied in Buddhist thought as the deity Mara. She questioned him fiercely, saying, "Who are you to be the enlightened one?" and, "Who do you think you are?" This voice of doubt might sound familiar.

In an act of great courage, the Buddha simply reached down and touched the earth. His response was a simple gesture, but it acknowledged the basis of being human. We are of this earth, we are born, and we will die. The first Noble Truth is translated as "Life is suffering," which is an easy way to remember it. And it is also a whole lot deeper. It acknowledges our imperfect perfection. It recognizes that we are impermanent, like all things in this temporal world. And it brings us to our commonality with all living things, above all else.

There is another notable part of this story—it would not be the same without the woman who made the offering. In the story, she goes to great lengths to milk the cows, make the rice, and provide sustenance. She didn't know why she was doing these things, she just did what came to her as an act of devotion. It is her golden bowl that she freely gives, full of richly prepared rice and creamy fresh milk. This invites the second Noble Truth that recognition of the suffering is where we start: "Holding to self-centered thoughts, exactly the dream." When we are caught in our own version of things, hung up on our insistent view, we suffer. And we cause other people suffering. Here we may need to show others the impact that a bad experience has on an actual person. We bravely convey their story to effect change.

The woman in the story of the Buddha acted from a place of generosity. Her heart was open and she moved in the deep course of wisdom, acting, serving, feeding, without pause or question. She offered everything, even the bowl, and it was not for her own benefit, but from a place of gratitude and compassion for another person.

"Each moment, Life as it is, the only teacher" is the third Noble Truth. Here we come back to a solid connection to two of our principles, Congruence and Synchronism. We trust in the inherent goodness of life and bring our attention back to this very moment, and allow life to teach us. This moment is where we can heal the missteps, miscommunication, the ways we miss each other by returning to the connection. We can choose to interject during the product planning meeting that's off the rails and over time, and so bring all of us back how this connects us to our goal, our mission to serve the specific needs of our users. I can humbly seek repair in connection with the director of product for the interjection if need be. This moment where it is, where you are, holds all the power and all the teachings needed for your life.

As this applies to research, we can notice if we are disconnected, and choose to reconnect. Connected Researchers can follow what is actually happening for the participant. We can enjoy the interactions and learn from them. We can let life happen to us and through us. We can be in this moment, with this person in front of us. We can acknowledge that all of this is a training ground, life is a boot camp, and we are the brave adventurers who signed up for this journey. It implies that the richness, the palpable, tangible, and often enjoyable aspects of life, those are the things that live right here in the present moment.

The fourth Noble Truth is a reassurance that there is a way out of suffering by "being just this moment" and that could also be read as "being with." It assures us that we have a way to connect with people by first acknowledging that we are all human, and that means we at times are all suffering. And when we insist on perpetuating the suffering, we make it worse for ourselves and others. But when we turn our attention to the present moment, returning to the here and now, we can make a choice based on our values rather than our reactivity. We can choose again. This liberates us and it liberates others.

Now that we have this framework established and have tied parallels with our mission in UX, we have revisited the Four Noble Truths from the standpoint of technology development.

1. **There is a rift between technology and the people it is developed for.**

Technology is made to be used by people but often, it is created in a vacuum and instead has harmful, unintended effects. There are at times aims of the business that are knowingly not in the best interest of the people who are using the technology.

2. **Further emphasizing the divide, we cling to our opinions that alienate others.**

By seeing ourselves as different, or more advanced and superior than the broader users of technology, we further alienate them and as a result, ourselves. We must consider the broader contexts of use and the societal, individual impacts of the far-reaching effects of technology propagation in our lives.

3. **Healing the rift happens now, in the moment.**

Now is the time to effect change and work on behalf of our users, our customers, and those who are suffering to varying degrees. This is not an abstract ideal or timeline, it happens in this moment we are in right now.

4. **In connection, we find compassion's way.**

Empathy is an active goal, not a concept, or a nice to have. It happens in connection and in an embodied way. To connect with others, we must also connect with ourselves. To connect with our users, we must connect with one another within our UX communities.

We know these are bold statements. Now is the time to be bold and lead with compassionate courage. None of us can do this in isolation, however, and this is why we are seeking to bolster community and awareness with others in our industry around these values and principles. We hope these words can encourage reflection and further conversation. Now that we have the fundamentals in place, the what, let us continue on to the how, the specific techniques that help bring the Heart of UX to life in practice.

PART III
THE HEART OF UX TECHNIQUES

PART III: THE HEART OF UX TECHNIQUES

MASTERING THE ART AND CRAFT OF UX

This section is dedicated to giving you specific and tangible techniques, skills, and tools for mastering your craft as a researcher. Some of these techniques are concrete, and some are attitudinal. These skills teach specific ways to live the principles of the Heart of UX, and are important and applicable in the moments of your life where you are conducting UX research too.

THE BIG WHY

The bestselling book *Start with Why* by Simon Sinek brought to the forefront the idea that living from your purpose is the most motivating way to live. For example, one woman who runs a $36 million-per-year company has a goal to reach $100 million per year in sales. Why would she want to increase her revenues? When interviewed, her biggest purpose was so that men will take her seriously.

We all have a reason for being in this burgeoning field of UX. Billions of dollars are poured into making better products each year, and we are all a part of a massively growing field that didn't even exist before 1990.

Your big why will reveal the reason you decided that this industry is how you want to spend your days. Your big why helps you get out of bed every morning, and keeps you going when things feel dim. Remembering what brought you here helps connect you with your aspirational, creative, imaginative, and open-minded self. It helps you connect to your purpose and brings you back into the equation of all the things that matter that day.

Your light is needed. Your specific purpose and personality are unique. This is the only time in history that you will happen, in this body, in this lifetime, with all of the circumstances and life lessons that have made you who you are. And when you infuse your work with your purpose, you become a powerhouse of grit and determination, delicately balanced with optimism and acceptance. Remembering your big why gives you focus, clarity and vision when you feel lost, and it is a compass that helps keep you on track.

Remembering Our Purpose

One day I had lunch with an old colleague of mine. As we sat together, chatting and catching up on our lives, this idea of purpose entered the conversation. I asked her why she chose the field of UX research. Her voice softened and deepened as she recounted her desire to advocate for people who are often discriminated against. As she remembered her original desire and purpose, I saw her energy grow, she felt more alive than before. We remarked on how our reasons for entering the field can sometimes get occluded by our to-do list, and as we suffer in the shadow of busyness, we forget. Remembering our purpose re-energizes us as researchers and designers alike to create a world where beautiful experiences abound. For my friend, advocacy is paramount to her. She was revitalized to help create products and be a part of teams that erase prejudice and malice, and has a keen eye for where blind spots show up on product development teams. Remembering her big why helps direct her efforts and fuels her day. —Jon-Eric

Exercise: Finding Your WHY

Here, we've adapted an exercise from Rod Stryker's book *The Four Desires*.[28] You will need a pen, colored pencils, and a journal or a sheet of paper. Begin by taking a few moments to write down why you or are interested in the field of UX in the first place. What was your motivation? Why UX? What did you hope to accomplish and what really got your blood boiling?

Now imagine a friend, family member, advocate or partner, someone that really knows and accepts you. See in your mind's eye how they have watched you grow in your career and life. Feel their care and support of you, and remember ways that they have helped you.

Now you will get into the part of this exercise that is thought provoking and evokes rich symbols from your subconscious. To do this you will write a eulogy: your own. But it will not be written from you, it will be written from the voice of the person that you imagined above, the person that supports and encourages and believes in you. This is a person that can see you clearly, and knows your intentions.

Imagine that you are this person, and have been asked to write a eulogy for you. Be rich in imagery as you describe your life. What did you accomplish? Who did it help? How did you transform yourself? How did you transform others? What really mattered? What differences did you make for the world, society, the planet? Did you have any regrets? From the perspective of a loving and caring friend, tell your life's story.

Now take out a different color pen or pencils and circle the key words. Circle words that jump out at you, words that seem to pop out of the page a bit. Look for themes, emotions, desires.

Look at the keywords you have identified and see if you can find a pattern. Write them all down side by side. Craft a sentence that includes all of your themes. It is important to make this sentence a present moment as well as positive and affirming. Stay clear of "don't" or negatives. Include specific imagery that makes it personal and makes you feel good. This is your big why. The sentence might be something like, "I travel the world, bringing nourishment to people across the globe," or, "I have a beautiful home, a loving family and enough to share," or, "I empower people by telling their stories." Whatever you have designed, put this sentence in a place you can see it and remember it often. Be refreshed by your unique and important purpose.

EXPERIMENTAL ATTITUDE

In our roles as researchers, we conduct experiments to better understand what is really happening. While this seems to go without saying, the willingness to "fail fast" should extend to the research itself, not just exist as a design expression that supports a method of testing. In Hakomi, we call this an experimental attitude, or possessing the ability to try things and be willing as heck to let it fail. Having an experimental attitude means that as a researcher, you allow yourself to be human, and take guesses. From how you set up the research schedule to the questions themselves, all activities are capable of morphing, evolving, or changing into a new form once we let go of the idea of needing to be right. Instead we embrace an attitude of experimentation and lightheartedness. This attitude gives us room to mess up, see when something needs to shift, and take action. Being willing to have an attitude that is not afraid to fail is at the core of the Heart of UX. Building the confidence and comfort to do so requires the rest of the psyche-building skills present in this book.

Here are some tips for the Connected Researcher:

- Set up the experiment in a controlled way.

  - People are not analogous to chemicals in a beaker. The correct setting is loving, not sterile. As best you can, keep the rhythm of the session trustable and repeatable, while still allowing for variances. For example, someone may spend more time on a task than you allotted, but the conversation that happens because of this can point to the real problem, and often the solution.

- Have a true experiment.

  - Come from a place of not-knowing and curiosity.

  - Start the person from a realistic point. For example, people don't come to a product knowing the designer's intentions. If the person needs to understand what is being offered and would normally land on the home page, let them orient themselves as they would in real life.

- Gather data—by facilitating experience.

  - Words aren't all the data. Body language, gestures, tone of voice, facial expressions, and other cues are all rich data sources.

  - Facilitate the person's ability to express what these cues really mean. Help them make the subconscious conscious by bringing attention to a gesture, expression, or glance.

    – As a note, attuned noticing, reflective listening, and making contact are facilitation skills. They are also experiments within the experiment. We will teach you these skills later in this chapter.

ATTUNEMENT: BEYOND SOMEONE ELSE'S SHOES

Psychotherapist Richard Erksine writes that attunement for psychotherapists is more than just knowing what another person is feeling—"it is an experience of being in their skin."[29] There is both a physical and emotional sensing of the other person's experience and a feeling of unbroken connectedness.

Attunement is both a kinesthetic and emotional sensing simultaneously. This state of attunement is something perfectly natural and ceaselessly occurring in us all of the time. As we learned in the first section, our brains, hearts, and bodies are sensing and feeling our world, to keep us safe and connected to others. It turns out that, to our mammalian bodies, connection equals survival. Making this explicit means that we can rely on our whole experience, body, heart, and mind, to give us the information we need to stay connected.

Connection + Compassion = Attunement

Having breakfast with a friend and colleague, whom I respect for being well-versed in attunement, I noticed how I kept looking away and breaking eye contact during several points of our conversation. It had been a long time since we'd seen each other, and so much life had happened and I guess I felt a bit nervous. I also had a full day of work ahead of me and I may have been preoccupied with what tasks were to come. After a while of talking and catching up, we had a moment of genuine connection and she said, "Well now I can feel my friend!" She was naming to me that there had been a slight rigidity or formalness that wasn't usually there. Her attunement had helped our connection to deepen into a place that went beyond small talk, to the more meaningful places that our friendship afforded us.

I took this experience with me into my day as I began conducting research sessions. I remembered her comment, and her basic human desire to connect on a deeper level, and let that inform me. I let my own skills of attunement shine forth, so the participants who I interacted with that day could feel that I was totally and fully present with them. And that gave us all a more satisfying interaction, which turned into enlivened data. —Jessica

ORIENTING

As a foundation of our ethics as researchers, we take safety as our first priority in any research activities. We always work in pairs when going out in the field, and avoid things like carrying cash incentives. We encourage our researchers to have a balanced schedule of interviews that keeps them nourished and happy, out of dangerous traffic times if possible, and we foster a commitment to ethical behavior in the workplace. So how do we extend this sense of safety to our participants and all who come into our lab?

In the most deliberate ways, it is important to establish trust and rapport as quickly as possible as a person embarks on the vulnerable journey of being asked to try a new gadget or technology that is likely unfamiliar to them. The technique of orienting can help establish that trust more quickly than if you jump right into the task at hand, forgetting that this person's nervous system needs time to settle in.

We start each and every research session with some basic orienting steps, noting any moments where we might need to pause, take a step back, and help a person take the time they need to relax into their surroundings. Orienting a person first to the new room they're in helps to create an immediate sense of safety. The truth is that when a person walks into a new space or meets someone for the first time, no matter how self-confident, there is a small stress placed on their nervous system. We want to create safety right off the bat, and orienting someone to their surroundings adds to a feeling of safety and calm.

We start by showing a person what to us is already familiar: "this is the webcam, microphone, and the computer you'll be using for the next hour. Feel free to look around and get comfortable. If you need it, the bathroom is down the hall to the left." What we have seen in practice is that while you go down the list and show that you're taking your time with them to do so, you are giving them permission to settle in, to take some deep breaths, and to become emotionally and mentally available for the task at hand. This builds a container of safety and lets the person know that you care about them as a human. This is an important technique for remote sessions as well, although the orienting details will be different. It adds great value to start off deliberately with a kind and slowed pace. Later in the book we have provided a basic script for orienting a person to a research session. Feel free to use this and edit it to fit your own activities.

REFLECTIVE LISTENING

The skill of reflective listening is common to many people who are interested in communication, and one of the most useful skills in the Connected Researcher's toolbox. This skill will unilaterally change both the way you do research and how you talk to others from now on. Reflective listening meets basic human needs to be heard, understood, and accepted. Oftentimes people repeat themselves because they do not feel a confirmation that they are understood.

At its most basic, it can literally be repeating word-for-word what someone has just said. You can preface it with, "What I heard you say is..." or just repeat directly.

When you have more comfort and practice with it, you can summarize several things they have said. The most important thing is to keep it free of interpretation and accurate. Do your best, and then be open to correction. Sometimes you hear inaccurately, and sometimes hearing their own words back helps people clarify their true feelings. This points back to our experimental attitude.

Tip: If you are afraid that you won't remember everything, it's okay to slow someone down and ask to clarify. Try saying, "Can I slow down around that for just a second? I want to make sure I heard you right. You said…"

Exercise: Reflective Listening

Decide who will be Person A and who will be Person B.

Person A:

- Talk for three minutes about a challenge that you overcame today, or this past week. Discuss something important and relevant, but not triggering or something too vulnerable.

Person B:

- Listen actively. This means repeating what you heard every so often, back to your partner. Do not interrupt, or add your own personal experience, even if you resonate and agree completely. Feel free to jot down notes if it helps you remember.

- Do not respond or add any new content—this point cannot be emphasized enough!

- Just listen, and reflect back what you heard. That is all.

- Do your best to repeat the words and phrases back to them, exactly as you heard them. Begin with the phrase "What I heard you say was…" Do your best to include as much important detail and thematic meaning as you can. See if you can reflect back what person A said as completely as possible. When you are finished, check back with person A. Ask something like "was there something that I missed?" or "was there anything else?" or "did that sound right?"

Person A:

- Correct anything that was missed, misheard, or misinterpreted by person B.

Person B:

- Reflect back any corrections that person A may have made.

- Notice what it is like to listen actively, fully, and to reflect back what you heard. Does it feel good? Connecting? Overwhelming? Difficult? Expansive?

Person A:

- Notice what it feels like to be heard. Was this different than a normal conversation? If so, how?

- Discuss.

Reflective listening has the powerful effect of allowing the speaker to feel fully heard. It is unusual for most people to be truly listened to outside of a doctor's or therapist's office, and so it has a side effect. The side effect is establishing trust, which goes along with our first two techniques, attunement and orienting. Reflective listening also builds rapport. In the hands of a Connected Researcher, this tool can amplify a research session beyond what the simple description can convey.

Just as we felt heard when attending to our inner critic in the exercise above, we offer this gift of active listening to our participants. Spontaneous joy, feelings of friendship and commonality begin to develop in the course of a research session. And what makes your participant feel good in turn makes you, the Connected Researcher, feel good too. Once you are off on the right foot, the session will have a felt sense, visceral and embodied, one that takes on new meaning for both you and the participant.

As is the case for many things, our bodies also record the interaction in the nervous system. You will have more detailed recall and a better grasp of what the person's main themes were from the session for your debrief and subsequent analysis. With reflective listening, you get a chance to slow down, to make sure you heard the person correctly, and fully. You get the chance to check out your biases or admit where you were distracted and try again. Your data is now verified, more accurate, and your recall precise. When we drop ideas of needing to be right, and assume the attitude of a curious witness who is willing to be wrong, make mistakes, and be corrected, our vulnerability brings people forward and they offer their truest truths.

ATTUNED NOTICING

Eye tracking research relies upon a specialized computer to precisely follow the eye movements of people looking at a webpage or software application to see where their eyes linger. The detailed outputs that this type of method creates are typically heat maps or gaze plots. The heat maps show us where people looked for the longest, and over the course of multiple sessions, we can see the main areas of what we deduce as interest. As a side note, guess where we've found that people's eyes go most of the time? To people's faces—especially their eyes. Recall our previous discussion on limbic resonance and you'll see that here, in action.

In truth, our human bodies are vastly complex systems of intricate networks, efficient beyond measure or reproduction. Our bodies are the most super of supercomputers. And so remembering to rely on your body—and its skillful signals of reading, intuiting, and noticing small clues to another person's experience—is always as available and accessible as your own heartbeat.

Attuned noticing (*adapted from "tracking for indicators" in Hakomi Mindful Somatic Psychotherapy*) is the practice of actively following a person's body and what it's expressing in the moment as a source of primary information. We all know that attending to gross body language will tell us volumes; 80 percent of interpersonal information is communicated via body language. We understand that although a woman at the café speaks French and we don't, when she shrugs her shoulders, she is communicating something about her feeling of being unsure at that moment. Attuned noticing is amplifying that skill, or giving yourself permission to study what bodies are communicating. Attuned noticing highlights that the body is unceasingly communicating at a subconscious level—and that these communications emerge all over the body, in subtle and brief ways. We see these small movements, gestures, and signs as a way for us to gain access into a person's reality, to get a glimpse of what it might be like to be that person.

These "indicators" are infinitely varied but may appear as:

- The slight twitch of the eye when a person is asked to respond to "how much would you say you spent on shoes last month?"

- A person is ever so gently holding their left ring and index fingers in their other hand, gently stroking them. This is a self-soothing gesture and indicates that they're feeling scared, sad, or anxious about something, but either aren't saying so verbally or are not consciously aware of it.

The Connected Researcher is continuously attending to, and curious about such indicators—these small signals in the background as they speak with a person. They know that the body is a continual source of information and so they lean into their natural curiosity around what the person's subconscious is communicating.

Through attuned noticing, the researcher attends to things like:

- Tone of voice
- Prosody (rhythm, inflection, emphasis) of their voice
- Subtle and overt body language
- Facial expressions

These signals enable us to ask better questions, informed by much more than a script or even what someone is saying verbally.

An important note: the safety of the attunement is an important piece. This technique is called attuned noticing because there is a basis of kindness, and an understanding that non-harming is our foundation. There is a difference in noticing a facial expression and using it against someone versus noticing a facial expression and using it to assist someone in a shared understanding of their experience. For example, we don't want to point out something and make someone feel self-conscious. This is much more subtle, effective and kind. It's more like saying, "I think I noticed something there, is that true?" The main thing is to be willing to be wrong, and to be corrected by the participant toward a more accurate reflection of their experience.

Attuned Noticing as a Pathway to Meaning

During an interview in Utah, I was conducting an in-home interview with a woman about her credit union. Jamie was in her late 50's, and her fair skin and hair were as neatly kept as her home. Although she was well put together, I noticed a discomfort in her face, especially around her eyes. I made a mental note to watch for this sadness, being sensitive to her feelings, and with the intention to see how I could best serve her humanness while there in her living room.

As a researcher doing field work, I am trained to first notice the surroundings of a person's workspace or home as clues to their general preferences and behaviors. As I looked around her home, I saw a picture of a young woman in her early 20's sitting close to the chair she was in. I commented on the loveliness of the young woman, and how happy she looked. Jamie offered that her daughter, the woman in the picture, was away on a two-year mission abroad. I saw the glint of sadness flash across her face and penetrate her eyes, wrinkling them ever so slightly at the corners.

I noticed that I could feel the sadness in my own body, and decided to take a guess. I named the sadness I saw. "Oh, you are missing her, huh?" At this Jamie's eyes welled up with tears and she admitted that her daughter had only been gone five days, and that she missed her terribly.

Following this attuned noticing, the resultant interview was heartfelt, connected, personal, and the depth of learning was unexpectedly rich for the stakeholders watching live through a Zoom meeting in Texas. The stakeholders knew that people make financial decisions based on emotions all the time, and that financial institutions have a responsibility to help their members use their money as they need to in their life. From this deep and practical interview, the company expanded their focus on families and in helping them to transfer money to each other more easily while traveling or abroad. This woman's willingness to share her story, and our connection, had a direct impact on how this financial institution helps families with their money.

Most of the time, the signal itself that we see—the flash across someone's face, the rise of heat in their body—doesn't tell us what is happening, just that there's something there. So once you notice one of these signals, how do you work with it? Often it may be enough to pause, make space and let the person offer whatever is arising for them. But you may also wish to take a more active approach. This is where the next skill comes in: making contact. —Jessica

---

Exercise: Jack and Jill Went Up the Hill

Pair up with a partner. Choose who will be the first speaker.

P1: Thinking of your day, tell the listener about something that happened to you today, but only use the words "Jack and Jill went up the hill." Convey your story with emotions, facial expressions or gestures, while only using the words, "Jack and Jill went up the hill."

P2: Watch as your partner tells you about their day while only using the six words. Although all you will hear is the repetition, what you will understand will be quite different. You may feel their emotions, understand the energy—was it amped, or low?—even glean the content of the story. You will be amazed at how much you can understand just by watching body language and trusting your intuition.

CONTACT STATEMENTS

Delivering a contact statement is a skill pioneered by Ron Kurtz, the founder of the Hakomi Method. Building on previous work from other psychotherapists such as Richard G. Erskine, Kurtz began using contact statements to make contact with a client—conjuring the image of an *ET* moment where the extraterrestrial reaches out and touches the finger of a boy with his own glowing finger. To make contact with someone is to create a connection with them, to show that you get them. To maintain the connection is to stay in contact with them, similar to a phone line, where even when you are not speaking, you can tell if the other person is on the other end of the phone.

To create a connection, the Connected Researcher demonstrates understanding. Initially, this often means following the details of someone's story and then reflecting the import of their story and its components back to them. This is the practice of reflective listening, introduced earlier. After an initial resonance is established, contact can go to a deeper place. And this is where the use of contact statements come in.

A contact statement is a short, simple comment about the person's present experience, often an underlying emotion or signal discovered by attuned noticing. The contact statement names the present experience or signal and brings the person into a deeper place, perhaps one they weren't even aware of consciously. For example, maybe the participant is having a hard time figuring something out as they talk through a task. The researcher says something simple, like "confusing, huh?" It's not necessary or advisable to clear up the confusion, just name it and see what happens from there.

Offering a short simple comment shows that the researcher is following what is going on for the participant. The person often feels relief, safety and ease as a result. Feeling listened to and understood, the person relaxes and goes a bit deeper. This brings a richer and more panoramic sense of the person's experience.

Contact is how you can connect with something you may have noticed, like a slight shift in posture, a repeated movement, or flare of the nostrils. You don't need to work too hard making contact; in fact, it's much more effective when you don't.

This also reduces your cognitive load by externalizing your hunches. When you notice something, you can make contact by making a short statement. This statement is an experiment of sorts: it's offered as a guess into the person's inner state, not a judgment or declaration. The person is free to agree or disagree. Either one is fine—it helps you clarify what is happening and gives you more data. To this end, contact statements are typically phrased as open-ended questions.

Here are some examples of contact statements:

"There's something about that, huh?"

"That's important?"

"You're thinking about something?"

"You're feeling something?"

"How was that?"

"How are you feeling about that?"

All of these allow an opening to something that may not have been otherwise expressed, or even made conscious. Contacting a person tells them that they've been seen and heard.

Contact vs. Leading

As researchers and designers, we have all been taught or at least heard about not leading the participant. Just like lawyers, not leading the witness is a vital skill. Delivering contact statements is different than asking leading questions. The questions we ask are important. This is as true during the interview itself as when we are writing the script, and determining tasks.

Sometimes designers want to see if the workflow they have designed makes sense. Instead of leading a person directly to the workflow in question, what if the person was allowed to explore and organically find their way to the workflow? This mimics real life and helps us see paths we could not have seen otherwise.

A leading question is one that subtly prompts a person toward an answer. If we were asking a leading question, we might say "Please go to the home page, and scroll to the middle and pick out a blue dress." Instead of that, you could ask the person "using this website, what would you like to do next?"

When we are taking a guess as a researcher, we are careful to offer this guess to a person, to be affirmed or denied. We are also noticing something that they said or did, something we feel curious about. We are not telling a person how to feel, or telling them how to do the task. Stay with open-ended questions, like "what do you think about this?" You are naming that you noticed something happen, then giving someone room and permission to talk about what is happening rather than just trying to accomplish a task.

Making contact with a person's experience and allowing them to explain or explore further is the essence here. It takes lots of practice and time, and we all make mistakes and ask leading questions. But this skill gives the researcher permission to acknowledge that they noticed something, and check it out with the participant.

SAVORING THE GOOD

In order to be present with others, you need to be resourced. Nourishment that will help you be your best self can come in the form of a beautiful meal, the right medicine, an artistic expression, an epic sunset, or a lazy day at the beach. Or it can be a very simple moment, like the smile on a baby's face. There are a myriad of forms that nourishment can take, and it is always available, in every moment.

It is a practice of a courageous and Connected Researcher to see the places where we forget to savor a good experience, and choose to turn our awareness toward relishing the moment. Think about the last time someone offered you a compliment. Consider if you replied with an exuberant thank-you and threw your arms around their neck—or you deflected the compliment, denied it, or brushed it off. It's often the latter, because we so easily deny ourselves nourishment all day long.

This is such a crucial technique to the Heart of UX approach, and one you can proactively practice all day long. The practice of noticing the good, as well as your own goodness, comes from actively intending to do so. You take on the idea that you want to notice the beauty in and around you. Starting small at first is helpful to developing the capacity to eventually be willing to contain more and more goodness, and more realization of our own goodness. This practice makes you a good researcher by adding fuel to your inner fire. Once you learn the art and joy of allowing yourself to be inspired by all of your surroundings, you will outlast the Energizer Bunny on the daily.

OUR DEEPEST FEAR
It is our light, not our darkness that most frightens us
Our deepest fear is not that we are inadequate
Our deepest fear is that we are powerful
beyond measure
It is our light, not our darkness that most frightens us
We ask ourselves, who am I to be brilliant,
gorgeous, talented and fabulous?
Actually, who are you not to be?

—Marianne Williamson

Soul Nourishment

From a physical standpoint, we understand nourishment as food and getting our basic needs met. And we can all usually admit that taking good care of ourselves by eating healthy meals on a regular cadence is advisable.

From a soul or psyche perspective, there are different ways to nourish yourself. One way is subjective and specific. The other way is not specific to one's actions or deeds, but through noticing beauty. Neither is better than the other. From the perspective of personality, actions, and talents, one way to feel good is to look for praise and recognition from others. The limit to this is that you are relying on another person to give you a compliment or make you feel good in some way about yourself.

But if you can rely on the beauty of your surroundings to bring nourishment to the inner parts of your being, you have a more readily accessible form of nourishment. Beauty is always available. The more you begin to notice it, whether it's nature or a painting or the glow of a computer screen, the more you will see. Your preferences matter here, and what you think is beautiful truly is beautiful. It can be quick, or fleeting, or just interesting, but the idea is that you are looking for symbolic food for your soul that excites or entices you.

Beauty is also a direct source to connecting you back to creative energy and flow. It is often the basis for gratitude, like when you stop your rant to exclaim "look at that sunset!" And for just a moment, the point you were making is less important than enjoying the spectacular color that fills the sky. All that has to happen is for you to notice it.

Beauty is within you and all around you. Think of a prism. A prism can take an ordinary room filled with light and make it a mesmerizing masterpiece of color. The light already existed, but the prism made it observable. This is how you begin to practice with nourishing your soul: keep it simple and notice what is immediately available around you.

In the grocery store, see all of the mountains of sweet fruit, the sea of color inviting hungry humans to dive in and truly notice the abundance. At the bank, notice the hard working people, and feel inspired by everyone's service, all at once. You notice as you drive that same highway you use every day that you can see the sky, and that warms your heart. It is all there and available for enjoying.

Exercise: Enjoy Life Fully

This exercise has two parts. The first teaches us about savoring, the act of enjoying something completely.

First, set aside five minutes to get quiet and close your eyes, and get a piece of chocolate or candy. Determine to eat only one bite, and let it last as long as you can. Before you put it in your mouth, notice the way your body already begins to salivate, in anticipation of the sweetness. Then place the chocolate in your mouth. Close your eyes as you slowly let it dissolve. Try your best to linger, and enjoy the sweet, robust and earthy taste as long as you can. If you like wordplay, think of words to describe your experience of the chocolate. See how your body feels as you enjoy the tastes and sensations.

Next, in order to explore the idea of nourishing your soul, we extend this savoring to something outside of your body. Find something simple in the person near you or in the room that is beautiful or pleasant. It might be the color of their eyes, the light coming through the window, the chill of your ice water, or a song in the distance that you enjoy. Anything you find pleasant will do. Choose something that has nothing to do with your performance or ego to help ground you in positive presence and a noticing that is not so personal. Let the experience of what you find pleasant extend as long as you can, and as long as it feels interesting. Just like you did with the chocolate, savor and enjoy whatever is around you.

Now see if you can keep enjoying the good feeling, or soul nourishment as you listen and interact with others. Notice the sparkle of someone's necklace, the twinkling lights on the Christmas tree, or how much you enjoy the taste of your coffee. We are actually taking good care of ourselves more often than we think, and letting ourselves have permission to take good care of ourselves is the basis for this practice.

This type of small, moment-to-moment noticing and enjoying will also help you stay energized, alert, and interested as you go from session to session, or spend countless hours designing your product. Staying connected to the things you find inspiring and beautiful is the same to the soul as eating three square meals a day is to the body.

Body Hacks to Quick Nourishment

If you are feeling stressed, scattered or depleted, try these simple exercises.

Power posing: Standing with your hands on hips in a superhero stance or with arms raised above will change the chemistry in your body. Turn your anxiety into strength, confidence and power with two minutes of power posing.

Grounding: Similarly, feeling your weight in the bottom half of your body helps slow anxiety and bring you into centeredness. Do chair pose, warrior poses or lunges, or lay on the ground to feel more grounded. You can also place your hands on your belly and feel into your center. When you need to ground subtly, just notice your weight in your feet and your seat.

Deep breath: Just one deep breath can take your nervous system from fight or flight into rest and digest. Inhale deeply to fill up your belly like a balloon, and let your exhale fall out like a long sigh. This can also help co-regulate anyone near you.

Exercise: Reflective Listening with Nourishment

Pair up and interview another person about nourishment.

Become mindful of your body, breath, and physical feelings. Make the intention to practice letting your soul get nourished.

Take turns telling each other about something that was pleasant, enriching, enlivening, or fun in your day, one person at a time.

> Make an attempt to accurately reflect what the other person is saying and expressing about what they enjoyed.
>
> Notice how you feel as you listen to the person talk about the thing they found pleasant. How does this affect you?
>
> Then switch and repeat the experiment.
>
> Discuss.
>
> How did it feel to interview?
>
> How did it feel to be heard?

Finding Inspiration

Inspiration is the stuff that connection is made of, the very fabric and thread of the ability to connect to another. When we actively take on the attitude that each person is inspirational, we open to finding inspiration in our whole day. Regardless of whether a person is at their personal best that day or not, there is always some hurdle they have overcome, some obstacle they have experienced, some challenge that they have risen to meet. It is our joy as Connected Researchers to remember this fact about people, and offer this perspective as a gift to the interaction.

This is also a direct path to empathy, and empathic connection. When you find inspiration in each session, your day will be filled with a lightness and respect for humanity that will nourish you deeply and keep you recharged for the next day. It is as simple as remembering to let yourself feel inspired by the person in front of you as best you can, and letting that feeling show.

> **Exercise: Finding Inspiration**
>
> In UX, we often say "check your worldview at the door." We also encourage designers and researchers to do a brain dump in advance of a study,

naming and bringing to light any known biases, ideas, hypotheses, and opinions. We will give you more to chew on about our biases in the next section, called Embracing Your Bias. For now, adding on to this wonderful and useful practice of owning your biases, we encourage you to take it a step further. This exercise will bring to light how to do that.

Find a partner to interview. The content of the interview doesn't matter as much as your own orientation. Don't read these prompts aloud, these directions are for the interviewer only. Keep the attitude listed below to yourself as you conduct three short interviews. Time each section for 1.5 minutes. Simply listen, say nothing while the other person talks, and try not to over act. Just follow the three prompts below, and note how your presence affects your partner.

1. For 1.5 minutes, ask your partner to tell you about their day. While you listen, take on the attitude and mindset of, "I need to get as much as I can from this interview, check all the boxes and remember all of the details! My worth is on the line." See what you notice about how your partner relays their day to you, and how you feel while holding this orientation.

2. For the next 1.5 minutes, ask your partner to tell you about their day again, and this time have the orientation and attitude that "There is a problem, and it's my job to fix it." Notice how your partner responds.

3. Take a short break. Close your eyes and feel into your grounded center. Then, come back to the awareness of your partner. For the final 1.5 minutes, ask your partner to tell you about their day one last time. Take on the attitude and mindset that this person is an inspiration. Look for beauty, both in the person and around you in the environment and let the world inspire you as you listen.

4. Ask your partner to tell you about those three separate experiences. What did they notice? Feel? Was it noticeable to them that you had different attitudes toward them?

5. Notice and write for three minutes about the difference you felt as you practiced this simple yet impactful attitudinal shift.

When we introduced this practice to a small group, the effect was pronounced. Not only did the partners who were being interviewed notice that the person holding the attitude shifted, they even knew that attitude that was being displayed, without the person saying anything. This goes to show that the way we see people, the attitudes we hold, and the places we assume all have an impact on the overall interaction.

SELF-CARE AND THE ART OF LIVING

Caring for your own personal body, soul and mind is not a new topic, and we have all heard of work/life balance by now. But often it is easier said than done. In our hectic pace, we seem to prioritize getting the work done versus how we get the work done. For example, in a classical model of a remote evaluative study, we might schedule thirty-minute sessions back to back and attempt to talk with ten people that day. We may not leave time for bathroom and water breaks for ourselves, or even forget to eat lunch.

As Connected Researchers, we work with the ideas of productivity and self-care in unison. We remember that although there are deadlines, there is also our need to enjoy each and every day of our lives, because this makes the best experience for everyone. Utilizing the Heart of UX self-care techniques, we set a pace that is more reasonable for our body. For example, a full day of interviews for us and our team includes a maximum of five interviews per day, with thirty-minute breaks between each person to take care of personal needs, debrief and refresh for the next session.

Self-care doesn't require a long time, unless you have neglected it, and is more related to taking small moments of nourishment on a regular basis than to what might feel like the indulgence in an activity or event. Self-care sometimes is as truthful as setting a schedule that is kind to your physical and mental needs in addition to the need of the project. It can mean bringing snacks or a water bottle out in the field, or saying no to a team dinner so that you can go home and take a bath. Self-care varies from moment to moment and person to person, so we can have an eye out for how to best care of ourselves in any given situation.

The realization that stress happens and that all life includes stress is likely not new to you. In fact, a manageable amount of stress actually helps us know that we are strong and can rise to meet any challenge. Time and time again, when interviewing people about times when they feel most alive, most people relay a story of overcoming challenges as a gateway to feeling satisfied.

We are not implying that you should reduce all stress and live a carefree life of frolicking on the beach collecting shells. Summoning our strength to overcome obstacles, to meet deadlines, and to participate fully in this modern life is purposeful and meaningful work. The point is giving yourself permission to keep yourself in the equation. When you are working on a deadline, and you have been holding your body in the same way hour after hour typing a presentation or report, it is self-care to take breaks, take a walk, play with your dog, or cut some flowers.

It is also self-care to keep trying to figure out what self-care is, and what it means to you each day. It is care to live your life in a way that gives others permission to treat themselves with the same kindness. To become a Connected Researcher and master the art of skillful moderation, we need to look at the ways we take care of ourselves in a regular and repeatable way. When we see these hindrances, we can begin to choose to let in the care instead, and find a new relationship within the cycles of life.

Artfully Seeing the Cycles of Life

Life emerges as cycles within cycles, and our work and our activities are no exception. For example, we have cycles on the project level, but also on a daily level or even a task level. Each stage can lead into the next and increase our awareness of our own patterns, meaning that we have richer self-awareness and skills. However, we often have interruptions or interference to the different stages that serve to keep us from becoming aware.

Often, we avoid certain stages for various, often subconscious reasons. In terms of UX and our work life, these cycles are important for us to notice. When we can see that we have a block in a certain area, or stage of the cycle, we can bring our attention to that block and seek resources to help us move forward. Rather than blaming ourselves, or trying to cover up a mistake, we can be deliberate and get support. Knowing that life moves in cycles, we can anticipate our needs for future cycles and work to make life easier by seeking support.

The basic stages of the cycles of any activity are:

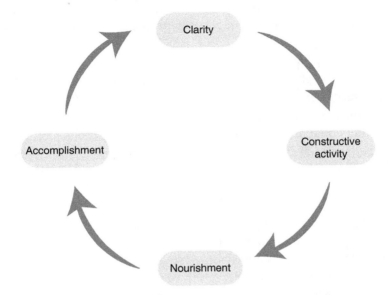

(*Adapted from the Sensitivity Cycle in Hakomi Mindful Somatic Psychotherapy*)

Clarity: Clarity springs from imagination. You get a big idea or suddenly you know what needs to happen. In research, this can be identifying a hypothesis, deciding on a hypothesis, or choosing an area of study.

Sometimes we have subconscious reasons for staying unclear at work under the surface, and unbeknownst to us. This causes an interruption in the cycle.

Interruption to clarity might look like feeling confused, foggy, stuck, or numb; not knowing what to do next; making poor choices; or relying on others to tell you what's next and not taking initiative.

Constructive Activity: Our clarity makes constructive activity possible. You know what to do, and you do it. It can feel super empowering. This is probably the most valued stage in our culture, but for some, taking action is difficult.

Interruption to taking constructive action might look like procrastination; never feeling quite prepared enough to do something; fear of doing things wrong; feeling pushed by others and resistant; being slow.

Nourishment: You can feel nourished by the outcome of constructive action. You did the thing, and now you are reaping the rewards. We are sometimes discouraged from receiving nourishment growing up, so we keep it out unconsciously or interrupt the cycle.

Interruption to nourishment might look like deflecting a compliment; having a "not enough" mindset; or not appreciating a moment like being alive on a beautiful day while the sun is shining and the birds are singing — and you are in your head about all you have to get done and don't enjoy the nourishment all around you.

Accomplishment: Letting ourselves feel the accomplishment of a task we have completed, before moving to the next task, is the activity of this stage. Feeling the effects of the accomplishment happens during rest. By resting, we give our subconscious brains a chance to shift out what was important, and we give our bodies, especially the nervous system, time to restore. This phase is hugely underrated in our larger culture, but it is essential for insight as well as health.

Interruption to feeling accomplishment might look like feeling tense, overly stressed, or busy; not taking breaks; jumping into the next task prematurely or skipping steps; quickly and regularly moving on to the next thing; thinking about work after hours; not being able to sleep.

By turning our attention toward the places where we get interrupted in our cycles, we see how we do things. This in turn allows us to let in more care where we need it the most. Becoming aware of where and how you interrupt your own cycles will create the fertile soil of learning how to deeply and mindfully take excellent care of your own precious life.

ACTIVE RECEIVING/LISTENING

Have you ever been moderating a session and noticed that the participant is a bit jumpy, and talking rapidly, or maybe over-explaining the reason they are not finding something? Sometimes this happens because people can feel that they are being judged or evaluated, even if they aren't. As a researcher, when you actively receive someone, be it their story, or what is happening in the interaction, it invites space for people to open up, and become more endeared to you. It calms their nervous system and activates rapport.

So what is active receiving? It is both active, having a quality of engaged, dynamic listening; and receiving, taking in, accepting fully. Let's break it down a little further. When was the last time you were around someone who made you feel good, like you were fully accepted for who you are, as you are? Maybe it was your grandmother, or your favorite pet—someone that absolutely didn't judge your morning breath or your messy hair, someone who listened fully and had nowhere else to be.

Remember a time when you told a story and everyone was captivated, listening with both ears and eyes? That is the feeling that active listening gives to the speaker. Oprah Winfrey says that underneath all of our motivations there are three basic questions:

1. Did you hear me?
2. Did you see me?
3. Did what I say mean anything to you?

In every interaction, we are silently asking these three questions, and a research interview is no exception. Our participants want to feel that they have been helpful, that their time and yours was well spent, and that they were appropriately recruited. This imparting of values comes from the quality of the interaction itself, not mere obligatory words of thanks at the beginning and end of a session.

To actively receive someone you must be engaged and active. You must step out from behind the one way glass and be a part of the conversation. Showing your interest, your surprise, and your curiosity invites more aliveness. Your orientation is one of awe and inspiration, as well as engaged curiosity: alert, alive, interested and asking questions to clarify.

Receiving is also a practice, and one that we don't do very often. Most of us swing from one side of the pendulum to the other until we make a practice of receiving. Practicing receiving means saying a full bellied, wholehearted thank you to whoever gave you something. It goes beyond that as well. It means really appreciating the wonder, the joy, the abundance, the story—whatever it may be. It also means fully accepting life as it is. There is a Zen saying, "Life as it is, the only teacher," which means that we say yes to what is, even if it's not what we expected. When practicing receiving as a researcher, it applies to our ability to accept someone, a participant or our boss, for what they do have to offer. It doesn't equal passivity, or saying yes to something you want to say no to. Instead it's more about receiving a person's whole story, messy and foreign as it might be.

Receiving looks like slowing down to offer a statement that shows that you have heard and you understand. It means offering care and abundant generosity to what a participant has offered. We live in a *not enough* culture, where most of the time we are subtly and not so subtly told that what we have been given is not enough. Actively receiving is a practice of generosity that turns this not enough thinking on its head. Receiving is a basic understanding that everyone is doing their best, even when it seems to you they are not. The world unfolds in luminous and generous ways. The magic is that when we practice actively receiving each person, we are more well-received and accepted as well.

Active listening is the Connected Researcher's way of practicing active receiving all day. The terms are very simple. First and foremost, keep the focus on the participant. In other words, don't add to their story, and use "me too" very sparingly. It's a subtle but powerful shift. Paired with making contact, actively listening feels to the speaker like they are finally being heard. And it builds rapport and safety very quickly.

Here are some key points:

- Pay close attention to what is being said, with words, expressions, tone.

- Instead of responding, reflect back what you heard. For example, "What I heard you say was ... (exact words if possible)"

- Try to only listen, speak only during your turn. Use pen and paper to write your thoughts while listening if you need to.

Paired with good boundaries, you can practice both actively receiving and having a good sense of how to disengage from taking on people's "stuff." In order to not get overwhelmed by their experience, you need to both receive them fully, and work with what you are receiving.

Receive a person fully and then let go completely, acknowledging each person you meet, the story they brought, the energy they had, the problems they face as well as their strength and possibility.

It's the Little Things

One funny way I now practice receiving in my life is to pick up every penny, dime, nickel or quarter I see. I have a bowl at home, and as soon as I return home each day, I enact a small ritual. I walk to the bowl, I bow, saying thank you to the universe for this symbol of abundance in the form of a coin, and then I place it in the bowl. This practice takes only a few seconds throughout my day, but reminds me often of how to receive. —Jessica

BOUNDARIES

> *"At the center of your being, you have the answer. You know who you are and you know what you want."*
>
> —Lao Tzu

Often, we choose our line of work because we are naturally empathetic, and we love to help people. We now have a common language in our culture about empaths, the people who take on others' feelings, and narcissists, people who can't put themselves in the shoes of another. We will not get into the details of that here, but we recognize that it would be harmful to suggest that people practice actively receiving without the equally necessary practice of honoring their own boundaries.

Boundaries exist on the physical level between you and the world. Your skin is a boundary that is naturally good and easy to recognize. Your skin separates you from the outside world in an alive and permeable way. We don't disintegrate because our skin, our biggest organ, is constantly navigating the separation between the things inside of us—blood, bones, and organs—and the things outside of us. Our skin is our first layer of defense, keeping out an abundance of bacteria and pathogens. But the skin is also permeable. If you put something on your skin, it gets absorbed into the body.

This is similar to our emotional life. Anger is a response to a boundary being crossed. Anger tells us that something out there happened, and it is not okay with something inside of us. And this is very useful to keep us safe. Something shifts in the way that we work with anger when we realize that anger is a response to a boundary being crossed. We can use this energy to help us determine the right action, and name how to care for ourselves as well as another person. Life is not a sacrifice. Being nice to someone else at your own expense isn't true kindness, because you are left out of the equation. Saying no is sometimes the best possible thing you can do.

"Boundaries exist so that I can feel you, and you can feel me." This statement of affirmation reminds us that boundaries are a good thing, a part of what it means to be human. As Connected Researchers, one of our biggest allies is the ability to define and respect our boundaries. To be trustworthy and open, we must honor and respect our own internal yes as well as no. One small example of this is starting and ending your session on time. As simple as it seems, it tells both your own nervous system and your participant's nervous system that you are respecting the arrangement that you've both agreed to. This is especially practical when doing ethnographic field work and entering people's homes.

Another way to honor this for yourself is to give ample breaks between sessions, no fewer than fifteen to thirty minutes between each session. This gives you a chance to refresh yourself and be available fully for the next person. You will be much happier at the end of the day if you have taken adequate breaks and nourished yourself often.

Exercise: Boundaries Meditation

The purpose of this meditation is to help you come back to your own center and know your boundaries. This can help if you feel scattered or too merged with another person.

Ground: feel your seat supporting you or the ground beneath your feet.

Notice how your body feels.

Rest your hands on your belly.

Breathe out with a sigh to relax.

> Repeat the mantra, "At the center of my being, I have the answer. I know who I am, and I know what I want."
>
> Bring your hands in front of you, and trace an imaginary and intuitive boundary around your whole body. See if you can feel where your boundary is. It might feel like a little bit of resistance. This is your bubble or personal space.
>
> Bring your hands all around to see where your boundary is above, below, and behind you, in all directions. Go slow. Let it be simple.
>
> Bring your hands back to your belly. Repeat the mantra.
>
> Know you belong to you.

We often do this quick meditation in the car, after arriving at the next interview. If you have a few extra minutes, this meditation helps to rebalance, especially if you have a feeling of merging with your participant's problems or difficult life circumstances.

It is no surprise that we are affected by our participants; after all, that is the point of empathy. As empathic researchers, we can often end up taking on other people's stuff, and sometimes the suffering of the world can feel overwhelming. This practice of returning to your essence, and reaffirming your own individual expression, helps you stay filled with energy and keep your personal sense of self. It can also be good when your brain feels full to overflowing with data. When you've collected all of the stories, needs, desires, and pain points of many people, it is often hard to begin to suss what is most important. This beautiful and simple meditation can help you remember who you are and where your voice matters in the big scheme of things.

Clearing the Air

A good practice to get in the habit of doing after a day of research is a clearing debrief. After noting your top takeaways from the day, take a few minutes to enact this ritual of completing the day.

Take a few moments to sit quietly and take a few deep breaths. Return your awareness to your body breathing and let the places within you which want to relax, do so.

One by one, bring each person who you spoke with to mind. See their face, their body, and acknowledge their humanness. For each person, let your body remember what was truly alive for that individual, and jot that down. After you've captured their main points, say goodbye to that person in your own way. It may be a bow, or a prayer or a wish or a nod, however it is that you say goodbye and thank you. Let go completely of each person's story. Return to your own true heart and thank yourself for the good work that you did today. Move out into the rest of your life free, fresh and clean of others' stories and needs.

GOING OFF SCRIPT

During our research sessions, we can often tell when a person is heading toward interesting material. We want to encourage them to stay in the experience and even spend some time there, maybe explore the thought, feeling, or sensation more than they would if they were just there to complete the task. This is where the idea of keeping the focus comes in. This is a bit like holding their place in line, while you encourage them to diverge and delve into a more subtle point.

Encouraging someone to divert from the task does indeed take a balanced approach. We want to "go with," and also realize that we only have a short time with the person. This often is less about what we hear in words or stories and more of a brief glimpse from our own intuition—a feeling or reaction that might be just under the surface for the participant. We are awake and practicing attuned noticing, and we have even taken a chance and tried to make contact with what we notice. Our job now is to give them the encouragement and acceptance they need to bring the thoughts they are having inside expressed out loud. For example, you may notice some frustration, but the person has not said it out loud. There are simple cues to give permission in a way that feels like an invitation rather than a demand.

These are trusty phrases and questions that you can use when the participant responds to a contact statement you have made, and organically goes "off-script." Remember, you are trying not to lead but to understand, deepen, and keep focus.

"How do you feel about that?"

"What are you thinking here?"

"Tell me more about that."

"What does that tell you?"

"What does that mean to you?"

"What are you seeing here?"

"How is that for you?"

"Tell me about a time when…"

"Show me how you…"

UNCONDITIONAL POSITIVE REGARD

Unconditional Positive Regard (UPR) is related to our first principle, Positive Presence. It's the active, intentional state of orienting toward someone with care and compassion, holding them in this positive frame without condition. When you feel this, it is nourishing in a way that is hard to define. We're so accustomed to gaining another's praise and acceptance in exchange for our performance that receiving these feelings from another person unconditionally is refreshing. UPR recognizes that no matter who this person is, what they've done or what they think, they are human like everyone else, with inherent basic goodness, trying their best on their own journey.

UPR was popularized by the humanistic psychologist Carl Rogers in the 1950's. Rogers was the founder of client-centered therapy, the notion of placing the client in the seat of insight, growth, and discovery. This was a big shift for mainstream psychology. Prior to this orientation, the psychologist or the analyst occupied this seat of expertise. They were there to explain things to the client from their education and expertise, and offer wisdom, more like a teacher.

Rogers held that "the individual has within themselves vast resources for self-understanding, for altering their self-concepts, attitudes, and self-directed behavior" and that these resources are brought into light when a therapist or practitioner holds up an unconditionally positive mirror.

Part III: The Heart of UX Techniques

He proposes that understanding, insight, and transformation are facilitated by and take place within the relationship, a by-product of the interaction of the core of a person's being with the practitioner that aligns themselves with this positive attitudinal orientation. We similarly view this as a central component of being a Connected Researcher. With positive presence onboard, an unconditional positive regard for each person arises.

UPR matches very well with our practices of user research, which place the participant as the expert or the seat of knowledge, with the researcher serving as the facilitator of the process. When practicing UPR, I am saying without words, by my face, body, and attitude, that each participant I meet has something to offer and is worthy of being seen in a positive light. Making contact with a participant's inner experience also gives you a way back to UPR.

Making contact with their state of being, however disruptive or difficult, gives you something concrete you can do in that difficult moment. And it tells the person that they are accepted, even if what they are experiencing is difficult. What usually happens is that the noticing that is offered is all that person needs to relax or move through that feeling. It helps you get back into a positive presence. This is very different from solving, offering advice, or pacifying. It is a deep regarding, with a basic belief in the goodness in that person.

As researchers, one of the hardest parts of our job is often that we must walk a very fine tightrope. It is our job to remain an objective collector of information, while simultaneously feeling and deeply understanding people to get at their actual needs and desires. The technique of making contact when supported by the foundation of UPR is such a freeing technique. It has given us something to do in those awkward moments when we don't know what to do.

It's possible, of course, that the other party may not wish to get so deep with us, or maybe that we don't want or need to connect so deeply with them as well. Even on a surface level, UPR feels good and it helps us to not judge and evaluate people. That in itself is worthwhile.

We now know from neuroscience that key mechanisms are at play with use of this technique. The two most notable that we've already mentioned are components of the principle of synchronism: limbic co-regulation and coherence.

When we actively foster feelings of appreciation, we enter a state of coherence, which then co-regulates another's limbic system to ours—and we are now in a state of resonance and connection with one another.

Cultivating Unconditional Positive Regard

How do you cultivate this attitude? Although it's seemingly simple, UPR is something that may take some practice to really feel proficient in. In some circumstances, it's easy. Think of your dog's face, or your cat, or a beloved relative. They don't need to do anything special for you to feel loving, positive feelings toward them. Now what about someone who is loud, opinionated, perhaps has different politics than you? Not so reflexive, perhaps.

We Were All Kids Once

One of the ways I cultivate positive regard for others is to try and see a person as the small child that they once were. This is especially useful if I'm honestly struggling with seeing them in a positive light for whatever reason. I imagine them playing with their *Star Wars* action figures, or running around the creeks catching turtles, screaming and laughing with their friends—whatever context I can see that person in as a laughing, natural child. This helps me see their true, in-most nature. It's completely happening in my own perception but it helps me get to a place where I can look at them without judgment or condition.—Jon-Eric

Try it the next time you have a conversation, it doesn't matter who it is. No one needs to know you're doing it. While you're talking, bring feelings of appreciation for the person to mind whether they deserve it or not. Note what happens in your body, in the ways you relate with this person. Keep trying it throughout the day as you remember to, and see what may be different about this way of interacting.

UPR and Remote Research

Is UPR only effective in person, or can it be applied effectively through remote mediums like online meetings? Based on our experience, we feel that it can be employed just as effectively remotely as in person. One does not need to be in person to experience the benefits and positive feelings of UPR. Could this be related to heart coherence? This is a phenomena researchers at the HeartMath Institute are currently gathering more empirical data around—investigating heart resonance at a distance as a part of their Global Coherence Initiative.[30]

We assert that your positive regard for another person is a worthwhile endeavor, whether you're in the same space together or miles away, connected via remote meeting. So don't hold back when conducting remote research. Continue to uphold a positive, unconditional presence for your remote participants as well.

ETHICS AND RIGHT ACTION

Now that your toolbox is loaded with all of the principles, ideas, skills, and techniques of a Connected Researcher, we can look to the ethical component of wielding all of those new super powers.

Understand Your Values and Ethical Guidelines

When we work with individuals, whether in a lab, on-site, or remote, we are partly responsible for our participant's wellbeing. From simple gestures, like offering water and showing where the restrooms are, to holding a person's personal details confidential, many ingredients go into building safety for participants.

Here are just a few ethical guidelines to consider during UX research:

- Keep a person's full name, address, and contact information confidential at all times.
- Represent the data precisely, when quoting—use exact quotes from the video or audio, not guesses of what you remember that the person said.
- Always obtain consent about what types of data you are sharing, whether it is quotes, videos, pictures, or more.
- Be honest about the purpose of your research.
- Do whatever you can to ensure the data is safe, and a person will not be contacted by a third party.
- Respect the participant's time and do not ask for more than the person has previously agreed to.
- Understand your own values and what you bring to the interaction. Keep your personal opinions to a minimum.

The Responsibility of Power in Research

As taught by Cedar Barstow in her book *The Right Use of Power*, in order to be appropriate with power, we must first own our own power.[31] While understanding your power as a good thing, one of your most useful tools is the ability to have an effect and influence the conversation. Even though we allow the participant to lead, and we put ourselves in a role of following, we must recognize that being the researcher puts us in a powerful role. In the Heart of UX, we understand that in each dynamic interaction, there is a person who has slightly more power and a person in a position that has less power. In this case, the researcher, because they are the ones capturing the data, is in the role with more responsibility of power, simply by being the steward of the story.

As researchers, we are responsible for accurately conveying the person's story and using this person's data for good. This puts us in a role of greater responsibility. When we recognize this and own it, we offer a much greater kindness to the dynamic of researcher and participant. In this position, we own the full responsibility to keep a clear and accurate account, to participate wholeheartedly and respect the other person's truth fully.

Know Your Role

In terms of a research session, knowing your role as a UX researcher helps keep the boundaries and expectations clear. It is also helpful to understand the difference between your personal power and your power being in the role of researcher.

An example of knowing your personal power is recognizing a situation that seems dangerous, or sketchy and making a quick exit. This is your own personal right and responsibility to keep yourself safe as a researcher. Your role power, on the other hand, is due to the fact that you are in a role as a researcher. As stated above, the role itself comes with power, and it is more compassionate to know this, plus know what role you are in. When you acknowledge that the role itself puts you in a place of power, you can be mindful of the power you wield. Owning this keeps things clear and safe for both parties.

Think of the more obvious example of a doctor and the role differential between doctor and patient. Because the doctor is in a role performing their job, they are in a position of power over their patients. Abdicating this position would be harmful to the patient, because they have sensitive and often private information about that person. If a doctor were to see her patient at the grocery store and ask her about her athlete's foot, that would be an abuse of power, based on confidentiality.

We are in that same boat while we conduct UX research. We are let into people's lives, their homes, and given confidential data—and knowing this is a powerful position helps everyone understand proper boundaries and feel safe. When working as a researcher, confidentiality of information is just one example of owning your power. Another nod to responsibly acknowledging your power is to remain professional and above board with your interactions. Knowing that just being the interviewer, and capturing a person's story, carries a responsibility and heft to it. The person feels your attention or inattention, and this is powerful.

BRINGING IT ALL TOGETHER

To summarize, as Connected Researchers, we:

- Embody engaged curiosity
- Learn and practice connection techniques
- Enjoy an attitude that appreciates
- Realize that we are all participating
- Are aware of our body, heart, and mind
- Are attuned to each other
- Have the highest regard for others (reflect their highest selves).

PART IV
EMBRACING YOUR BIAS

EMBRACING YOUR BIAS

By now, we have explored the science behind connection and what is happening in the brain, heart, and body as connection happens. We've defined principles, concrete attitudes, and orientations that can help us learn and remember who we are as researchers. We have gained the skills from tried and true techniques to navigate the waters of capturing and relaying people's stories with more precision. Now we will do something quite bold. We assert that through fields like Appreciative Inquiry and quantum physics we can now claim and direct our impact.

As we have mentioned, researchers are taught to attempt to be unbiased. But as we will explain, we know that we have an effect, just by observing. Our bold new perspective is as an observer with a role—embrace our bias and move forward with intentional positivity. Here are some ways that people are enacting such boldness in the world today that supports our claim.

APPRECIATIVE INQUIRY: QUESTIONS ARE FATEFUL

Much of what we encounter in the UX field is based on a well-worn problem-solving approach. The basic assumption is that people have problems to be solved and that product or service improvements are a logical outcome of these solutions.

A typical arc of this viewpoint looks something like:

1. Identifying problems and deficiencies
2. Analyzing the causes
3. Analyzing solutions
4. Developing an action plan

We as UX researchers spend a lot of time at steps 1 and 2. Finding and analyzing the causes of problems is something we're really good at. It keeps designers and product managers coming to us with their hypotheses of why something's not working, and asking for our help to find out more.

There's undoubtedly value to the answers and insights we provide in these interactions, but we need to take a step back and ask ourselves about the impacts of reflexively spending so much of our energy looking for problems. How does this orientation influence the kinds of data we're collecting? How does this inform our interactions with participants?

We propose to see what is instead possible if we look for what is already working well, or has worked well in the past. We use what Appreciative Inquiry calls the "positive core."

Appreciative Inquiry (AI) is a method we've been integrating into our research projects as a way to mobilize friendly curiosity, creative imagination, and enlivened design thinking. It produces clear next steps, results that are all based on strengths instead of problems. We've found the results of doing so to be far-reaching, some of which include more engaged and imaginative participants, fluid cross-team cooperation—and most notably, alignment for everyone involved.

AI is based on the work of David L. Cooperrider, Ph.D. It is traditionally applied in the context of organizations of all kinds. It has been used across thousands of groups around the world, including Apple, Google, Walmart, the United Nations, NASA, and British Airways, to name just a few.

The Appreciative Inquiry Handbook, by David L. Cooperrider, Diana Whitney, and Jacqueline M. Stravos, defines AI as "the art and practice of asking questions that strengthen a system's capacity to apprehend, anticipate, and heighten positive potential."

The Affirmative Question

AI holds that people and their conversations *are* the organization, and it's for this reason that so much emphasis is placed on choosing questions rooted in a positive core. This orientation is due to the following principles:

- Change happens the moment a question is asked or a statement is made.
- What we believe to be true is informed by and evolves through conversation.
- Our beliefs and perceptions influence our conversations. The opposite is also true.
- Whatever we are anticipating, we are likely to encounter. Our expectations form what we look for, what we see, and what we hear.

The Research on Word Choices

This isn't just being positive and talking positively for the sake of the rainbows; many businesses find that this also makes good business sense—in addition to employees feeling better and being kinder to each other—which are both worthwhile goals in themselves.

Example 1: Marcial Losada and Emily Heaphy, psychologists who studied organizational teams as a part of their research looked at, among other factors, the impact our conversations have on team performance.[32]

They measured impact by looking at:

- Profit and loss
- Customer satisfaction
- 360 reviews

The results of their research show us that the types of conversations we engage in have a direct effect on the performance of the whole team. In the following chart, you will see the ratio of types of conversations (such as positive vs. negative) to the effect on performance measured. High performance teams were teams that were found to have a high success in customer and employee satisfaction, as well as profit.

For example, take a look at the first row in the table. High performance teams had an instance of 6:1 positive to negative conversations, meaning that out of seven conversations, six of them were positive. Low performing teams had the opposite trend, only one positive conversation in twenty-one.

Type of Talk	High-Performance Teams	Low-Performance Teams
Positive to Negative	6 to 1	1 to 20
Inquiry vs. Advocacy	1 to 1	1 to 3
Self vs. Other	1 to 1	30 to 1

What we see here is striking and, if you've been around the corporate culture for any length of time, these findings will make intuitive sense. Positive, growth-oriented, cooperative, complimentary talk has a considerable impact on overall performance. In our research consulting business at Progress User Experience Research, we partner with many design teams that are both highly functional and enjoyable. Some of our clients have a weekly game day for the employees where they gather the whole team and play games like Pictionary together. Teams like this offer us the chance to work with people who are respectful, complimentary, and include us as part of a team. We see the beautiful products they design, and the fun that everyone has at doing it. The reward of such a functional and happy, cohesive group is far reaching and makes going to work with them easy.

Here's another example from one of the premiere relationship scientists in the field today, John Gottman. In his seminal and ground-breaking work, Gottman and his team predicted, with 94 percent accuracy, which couples would still be married within 10 years of visiting his lab.[33] He accomplished this remarkable feat by video recording 15-minute ordinary conversations between the couples and counting the number of positive and negative interactions between the subjects. He then determined the ratio of positive to negative and found that a magic ratio of 5:1 positive to negative statements predicted a thriving, lasting marriage. So whether in marriage relationships, work relationships, or any relationship, we see the power of positive interactions and positive presence is the glue that holds teams together.

The Basic AI Process: 5-D Model

Appreciative Inquiry follows a movement that should seem very familiar to those who have participated in or facilitated design sprints. It's an iterative, generative group process that begins with research and ends with design and implementation steps. Note that some models of the Inquiry have only four steps, combining both the Define/Discover phases into one.

Let's look at each of these five steps in a bit more detail. All of this information, and much, much more can be found in the book *The Appreciative Inquiry Handbook: For Leaders of Change* by David L. Cooperrider.

PART IV: EMBRACING YOUR BIAS

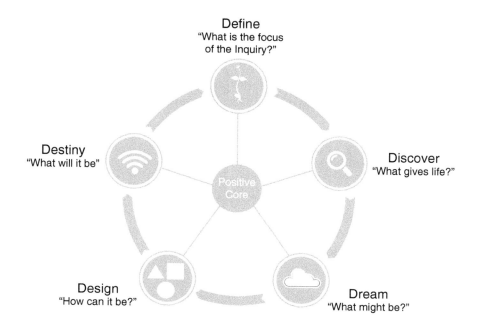

1. **Define**—"What is the focus of the Inquiry?"

Something has propelled the organization to decide to undertake the AI process. This is where a small, strategic team comes together to choose the topic. Working with a steering committee—typically composed at least partly with the project stakeholders—we agree on the aim of the inquiry. Focus is key, so that there's something everyone can align with.

Key features:

- Topic choice is a fateful act. The initial intentions of the inquiry agreed to at this stage will dictate the result.

- People commit to topics they help develop. Co-creation is foundational to the AI method. As many people as possible are asked to participate in the process, from beginning to end. We all have been in the position of being handed a new direction. How does that feel in comparison to something you had an active part in creating?

- Organizations move in the direction of inquiry. Just as topic choice is fateful, so is the direction of the question. Answers to questions dictate the subsequent design phases, and designs become implemented as concrete actions.
- Topics are affirmative or stated in the positive. Questions are explicitly positive. This keeps us focused on creative, generative ideation instead of getting mired in problems.

2. **Discover**—"What gives life?"

During this phase, we co-create the questions that will be asked as components of the inquiry. Questions are, once again, rooted in a positive core and are designed to elicit moments of peak performance or experience. Answers can come from any area of a person's life.

Key Features:

- We design and ask two types of questions: "best past" and "future images."
- All people participating in the inquiry interview one another, using these co-designed questions.

Again with the steering committee, we craft the questions that will be asked during the broader inquiry. The co-crafting of these research questions is an experience that builds cohesion for the steering committee and further ensures a collaborative project. This virtually guarantees that the results of the effort will be valued and hopefully carried forward.

Now we arrive at the really compelling part. After some brief training on interviewing technique, questions are offered in a one-on-one interview format, with everyone taking turns as both the interviewer and interviewee. Ideally, just about everyone in the company is participating. The idea is to have people speaking with one another in a way that is connecting and authentic. This in itself is a truly transformative experience. Watching people interact with a co-worker in this way is a beautiful thing to see. There's lots of laughing, and sometimes crying, and always something new learned about the other person. We've witnessed first-hand as people who previously presented as stern, staring at a laptop, and checked-out will suddenly come to life.

We researchers easily take this kind of experience for granted, but it has a powerful connecting effect on people, one that is often a surprise. Imagine the far-reaching effects this would have on an organization if just this alone were the exercise? People who have worked with one another, perhaps for years, without interacting personally would suddenly connect in a personal way. This is a powerful tool for eliminating barriers between colleagues—and all in the service of the organization.

The next step is to take all that fresh research data and look for trends. This begins with the interviewer/interviewee pair comparing their notes to see what commonalities exist between them. Then one of the pair offers these trends out to the group, someone starts doing that familiar post-it note dance and voila, we have an alive, mutually co-arisen and agreed-upon dataset of values to take into the next phase, dreaming.

3. **Dream**—"What might be?"

Now we take this rich set of data, all built on strengths, and move into the fun, creative phase of un-restricted dreaming. As small teams, we use the momentum that's been built and start playfully coming up with ideas, as free of judgment as possible to imagine what may be. Ideas are freely shared across this group and can take any format, from written ideas, drawings, or anything to get the idea across. This is another step where there's lots of energy, laughing, and excitement. This is just the kind of energy from which enlivened designs emerge.

Key Features:

- Freeform idea generation.
- The idea is to get into a state of flow and play.

In the dream stage, we want to imagine a future rich with strength and possibility. Envisioning what might be from the strengths of what exists, we craft vision statements that will guide our design for future stages.

4. **Design**—"How can it be?"

In the Design phase, we break up into small groups and, through creative play, we sketch, make a skit, write a haiku, or storyboard out an interesting, image-rich and compelling version of our vision statement of what the future state looks like based on our themes from the previous phase. The form can be as silly or expansive as desired, the only requirement is that the design includes the themes that came from identifying stories and our strengths.

Key Features:

- Designing and communicating ideas.
- Choosing the most stimulating design ideas.

Here, in an interactive afternoon, groups act out skits, write hilarious news reports, use scissors, feathers, pipe cleaners, and glue to build a mosaic—whatever the small group decides. The Design phase is about co-constructed versions of the future, all grounded in the reality of shared strengths. Ideas are then shared with the entire group participating in the Inquiry. The best ideas are voted upon and move forward to the final stage, Destiny.

5. **Destiny**—"What will it be?"

This is where it gets real. Using all of the energy of the day, as a group we focus on making these dreams a reality. During this phase, agreements are made and tangible next steps are planned out. It consists of activities that help create an overall strategy for implementation by assigning and taking responsibilities for concrete actions.

Key Features

- Implementation timelines and accountabilities. This phase can employ activities like prioritization exercises or putting tasks straight into a tracking platform.
- At this final phase we can look back to the Phase 1, Definition, and see how the focus of the inquiry has become destiny. Positive questions have resulted in a mutually designed, creative approach that has buy-in from a large contingent of people across the organization.

AI and UX Research

Although AI was originally envisioned as a technology to facilitate change in organizations, we've found integrating AI techniques and principles into UX research to be highly beneficial, and doing so has had a transformative effect on how we interact with our clients and participants.

We've found that our interactions with people, both clients and participants alike, are more fun, engaging, and we're able to ideate much more easily and effectively as we're coming from a place of collaboration and vitality.

We're encouraging others in this field to explore not only learning about and implementing AI but to **consider the power of a question**, especially in the fertile context of imagination and design.

Get Started with Positive Framing

An approachable way to try this out for yourself is by using a technique taught by AI called Positive Framing, a way of intentionally shaping a conversation to focus on a desirable outcome and energize others toward positive results. This encourages creativity, curiosity, imagination, and engagement by taking any negative, deficit-based frame and transforming it into a positive frame.

Positive Framing has three steps:

1. **Name it**—What is the problem, the issue, or the thing you don't want?
2. **Flip it**—What is the positive opposite? The thing which you do want?
3. **Frame it**—What is the desired outcome if this positive thing is true?

Try out this technique the next time you hear someone, even yourself, speaking from a negative, deficit-seeking place. With your self-awareness on board, notice the effects on the body, your energy, their energy, and what may now be possible to achieve what it is desired.

Here's an example of how this may work in a research session with a participant. You hear your participant say something like, "I would never use this as a sign in for this app, and I'm already turned off to it. It wants to connect with my Facebook account and import all of my contacts, my posts...everything? You've got to be kidding. I hear there's lots of people out there trying to get into accounts and steal things. I don't like it at all."

Okay, the negative thing is pretty clear, so let's begin with the Naming step. Using your reflective listening skills, you may say something like, "I hear that the security of your private account is really important to you and you feel like this is asking for too much permission, is that right?" Look for affirmation that you got it right and didn't miss anything.

When you affirm that you've captured what they don't want, move to the Flip step, where you now name the positive opposite. You might say something like, "So what I hear that you do want is a way to log in that doesn't require access to your private accounts, like Facebook. Right?" Again, check for agreement.

So now we have a conversation rooted in the positive. You can ask the participant to name the best positive outcome, or even ideate together about it, moving into the final, Framing step. That may sound something like, "Tell me how you would like to see this work instead, allowing you to sign in easily while also keeping your personal data safe." And then off you go, this time in a positive, creative direction, from which it's much easier to dream solutions together.

By owning the responsibility for the questions we ask as researchers and especially, the way we ask them, we enter the stream of reality where the strength of a system creates the most positive and effective change. We reverse our old ways of thinking from a problem-based to a solution-focused approach, and open to a new realm of possibility.

THE INTENTIONAL OBSERVER EFFECT

The discipline of psychology emerged from the milieu of the many other sciences that were on the rise in the 1920s. While Einstein was making his discoveries on the nature of light and energy, down the road in Vienna was Sigmund Freud and his famous red couch, where discoveries were being made about the unconscious. Both men fundamentally changed the way we view ourselves and how the universe works.

Psychology, in that pre-neuroscience era, had a problem, however. It was not possible to measure the unconscious, emotions, or any other psychological phenomenon. Does the ego occupy more brain matter than the id? Where exactly is neurosis?

As a result, it was often labeled a "soft science." This led to a kind of "physics envy," where the nascent science of psychology tried really hard to formalize, seeking measurement and the predictive certainty enjoyed by chemists, physicists, and mathematicians. Turns out that it's not easy being a social scientist in a room full of starched lab coats. What are you objectively measuring, anyway?

This is the genesis of many psychologists trying so desperately to achieve this validity by separating themselves, and their own psyches, from the phenomena they study, viewing psychological events as measurable, discrete events that can be quantified.

How is this relevant to UX research? Let's continue with the history a bit further.

A new branch of psychological study emerged in the 1960s. Human factors is the systematic study of the interactions between humans and machines. From human factors sprang the discipline Human-Computer Interaction (HCI) in the 1970s as computers became more and more a part of our lives, even if they were still communicating with us via punch cards.

From HCI emerged usability engineering, sometime in the 1980s. Note the "engineering" suffix, getting pretty rigorous, right? Usability engineering was the Big Papa of "User Experience," a term we started to see in the mid-2000s or so. So now we have UX research as a discipline and one of its more visible hold-overs from HCI, the one-way glass, put in place so that we may watch our subjects objectively, separately.

A Connected Researcher may well ask, "Why do we need to have these glass walls keeping us separate from those we're hoping to connect with?" We contend you don't—and that in fact, the use of them should be avoided if at all possible.

But what about those stakeholders? They want to watch the sessions. With the ample availability of High Definition video and audio, one can achieve a much better observation experience than one-way glass, all without the imposing mirror and people sitting behind it.

Behind the Looking Glass

I remember how this felt to me as a freshly graduated intern working at my first usability engineering consultancy in 1999. I was trained to seat the subjects inside the lab space while I was on the other side of the one-way glass with a microphone into the room. I would tell the subjects when to begin the task and they would tell me when they began and ended a task, to record the time on task measurements. They were also asked to think out loud while they worked. I sensed how uncomfortable people were in this environment. How could they not be? Talking to yourself in a stark beige room, clicking on some website while a kid in his 20's told you what to do from the other room. Oh, and you're being recorded. Oh, and there may be even more people in the other room snickering at how badly you use the mouse.

I knew this wasn't right. It didn't feel good. I asked my HCI-trained colleague why we did it that way. He said, "We don't want to influence the subject with our words, our body language, our tone." He and others were saying that simple non-verbal indications can soil the pristine container of data and make someone do something they wouldn't normally have done.—Jon-Eric

While we are indeed careful not to lead a participant, we now embrace a more holistic approach. We avoid sitting a person in a sterile and unfamiliar room by themselves and making them feel like a lab rat. We feel this isn't giving us the best data. We have moved away from trying not to have any effect at all and moving on to realizing that we do.

Clever Hans, Mind Your Hooves

Considering our assertions around being an intentional observer, let's focus for a moment on the first word: intentional. Being intentional means being aware of our bias and how we may influence one another. There are many subtle ways that we can unintentionally influence our participants (this is why two-way mirrors exist in the first place.)

Probably the most famous example of unintentional influence was the 1907 case of Clever Hans, a horse famous for being able to solve mathematical and other complex problems. Hans would be asked a question and then, to the amazement of the crowd, would stamp his hoof correspondingly to provide a correct answer. Was this an example of the evolution of animal consciousness?

Enter buzz-kill psychology to investigate what was going on with the apparently savant equine. Psychologist Carl Stumph observed that Hans was responding to the very subtle body cues that his trainer Wilhelm von Osten and others were broadcasting. As Hans would begin to stamp his foot in answer to a question, the trainer would tense as the correct answer was near. Turns out, Hans wasn't solving problems, he was reacting to those around him. Horses are incredibly empathic creatures, bred over centuries to be attuned to the emotional and bodily states of humans. This is not to downplay what Hans was able to do. His demonstration was indeed incredible, it's just that his feats were relational, not cognitive.

Wilhelm von Osten and Clever Hans

What Stumph had discovered was an example of the observer-expectancy effect, whereby a researcher's bias subconsciously influences a participant. This can cause signal-noise confusion and attribution errors in our research.

We should again remind ourselves that research participants are often in a heightened state of arousal. They're being evaluated and watched in an unfamiliar environment. They're absolutely attuning to you, the researcher who is their connected, safe person. So how can you downplay the effects of this kind of unintentional bias without placing yourself prophylactically behind glass? By being mindful of your impact on those around you. Here are some specific tips:

- Your participant may very well be looking for your approval as they seek to do a task the right way. Be aware of your smiles or shrugs in response to what the person is saying and doing. These subtle cues may be influencing their behavior and feedback.

- Avoid overt physical gestures that are related to what the person is doing. If their finger is hovering over what you consider to be the desired design target and you start typing or writing in your notes before they do so, they may see this as confirmation that they're on the right path.

- Note how you say things. Positive and negative intonations can change a person's response to your questions. You don't need to speak like a robot, but try to use a tone of voice that's friendly but not leading in one way or the other.

Schrödinger's Cat and Jakob Nielsen's Dog

Where Freud and Jung brought form to the psychology of the human soul and the landscape of the subconscious, Werner Heisenberg brought us deep into the apparent weirdness of the quantum landscape and its far-reaching impact on the experimental method. He discovered the "observer effect"—the idea that when you study a thing, you change it. By the very nature of observation, we have an effect on what we're observing.

Schrödinger took this already weird observation to an even weirder level with his thought experiment illustrating this effect. His experiment places a cat in a box with a poison gas machine only Sherlock Holmes' nemesis Moriarty would appreciate. The setup is this:

We have a radioactive element that emits a particle according to a known period of decay. If a Geiger counter detects this particle, it triggers another device that breaks open a vial of poison gas, killing the cat.

We don't know exactly when the particle will be released, just that it will at some point. So, we have the cat inside this box with this machine. From the outside, we don't know if at any one moment the cat is alive or dead. Either could equally be true. In quantum physics, this is called a superposition of states. At this moment, the cat exists in both states. It is both alive and dead. The field is sown with possibility. If we open the lid of the box, this field collapses, as we now see either a live cat very eager to escape the box, or a poor poisoned feline. Now that we know and our binary discovery is made, we have the answer. It is yes or no, 1 or 0—where before, both possibilities existed simultaneously.

What does this have to do with UX research? The cat represents what can be thought of as an objective truth. It is something we feel exists out there that we as researchers are charged to find and turn into a story to report back as evidence for making decisions. Our job is to look for closed boxes, open them, and see what's inside and when we do, we become part of the story we change it with our presence. So if we know we're going to have an influence on people simply by connecting with them, why not do so with intentionality? Harness this fact and use it for the good of the research and the good of the person there before you.

Here's a scenario to illustrate how this might play out in practice.

The Intentional Influence of Compassion

I have an in-lab usability research session scheduled for 1 PM. It's 12:55, so I go to the lobby to greet my participant, Linda. She just raced through rush hour traffic and experienced a difficult parking situation to get there on time. Flustered and slightly out of breath, she sees me approach her, and I can already tell she's experiencing stress in her system. I walk with her to get her a drink from the nearby snack room, asking her about her morning, and mentioning, "Isn't the blue sky beautiful today?" Already she can feel my sincere desire to build some rapport. We enter the lab, equipped with one-way glass, bright lights, and a camera. I can only imagine what goes through Linda's mind. "Of course there's a mirror wall ... I'm going to be grilled while a bunch of people watch me look stupid and my hair is a mess."

For this exact kind of scenario, one of the first things I do is assure people with some primary safety-making to help calm their aroused nervous system. I do this with my presence and my words. I may say something like, "There's a one-way glass as you can see, but I'm going to be in this room with you the whole time." Her system settles a little. She won't be alone under the bright lights. At least someone friendly will be there with her.

By this time we're seated, and the next thing I'm going to do is to orient her to the environment. This builds more trust between us and shows her that I'm willing to take the time to slow down and help her do this at her own pace. "You're going to be working on this computer. Here's the microphone, and a camera. I'd like to record our conversation so I don't need to take so many notes and can just focus on our conversation. Is that okay with you?" Now I've shown her my cards. I'm recording and I've also asked for her permission. I'm not going to try to take or get away with anything. This builds trust. More settling in, together.

Have I influenced the participant? Yes. I'm intentionally connecting with her on a personal, emotional, and subconscious level, and to what result? She's calmer, more settled, less self-conscious, and ready to focus on the questions at hand in order to explore this design together. I've intentionally attended to my own nervous system to cultivate a calm, relaxed, and reassuring demeanor in myself. I've also implemented the practice of unconditional positive regard. Through the co-regulation of our limbic systems, her limbic system is resonating with mine and calming down. There is increased trust, and increased oxytocin, which results in more trust and more shared empathy.—Jon-Eric

Acknowledging Our Bias from the Beginning

Here's a real-world example of how we work with bias, from one of our interactions with a consulting client.

An online marketing company asked us for our help to find out more about why people were canceling their automated newsletter service. In working through the study plan, we realized we had a bias that had emerged in how we approached the design of the research. We discussed the reasoning for this extensively and decided that it had some merit and may point to something that had not yet been discussed amongst the project team. Instead of watering down the study design for the sake of reflexive objectivity and moving forward, we decided to claim the bias and bring it to the client, prior to beginning the research.

Our meeting request invited interesting, robust conversations with the stakeholders as we captured all of our pre-existing opinions and beliefs about the product offering. Like emptying the dustpan so we can start with a clean sweep, we encouraged the thoughts, beliefs, opinions, limitations, and strengths of the entire team to come forward. We now had a shared vision of which way to point the research effort as we moved to the data collection phase of the project.

Working with bias can take extra time, and so we scope for this as part of the planning and organizing phases of a project. Whenever possible, we advise holding a half-day or full-day facilitated conversation to gather all of the biases, opinions, ideas, and suggestions upfront. Owning our biases relies on a willingness to take a step back and be vulnerable and is well worth the investment of time and energy.—Jessica

---

Bodily and Emotional Bias

> *"The emotional state we're in directly shapes the nature of information processing. The actual manner in which we store our memories and perhaps even think our thoughts is embedded in our nervous system as a probability function. This plus our emotions influence the unfolding of thought and memory, it becomes a state dependent process."*
>
> Dan Seigel, *Aware*

As researchers, we can see how our emotional state, our ground of awareness, directly and tangibly shapes our information processing. It affects the way we see and report what we experience.

Information co-arises with us in the field of perception. As instruments of perception we process this information, synthesize it, make meaning and memories—all formed by the ground of our emotional state and by the state of our bodies.

Our thoughts exist as wave functions, inexorably linked to the state of our emotions, our bodies, and our state of being. Our very thoughts, therefore, are different based on how we feel. The way we interpret the field of data, the possibilities of what is and what can be, is shaped by this. What would our research sessions look like, then, if we're feeling relaxed, open, engaged, and curious? We're broadcasting this good feeling, calm and open. The participant is co-regulating to our feeling. Does this change what is happening? Does this change the outcome of the research? Absolutely yes.

The cosmos in which we live is not only participatory, it is responsive to us and how we are in the world.[34] Research outcomes, therefore, are directly shaped by our intentions, feelings, and aspirations. Our findings and recommendations influence and bring physical shape to products and services, directly impacting the lives and experiences of both people and planet. How we show up in the world matters a lot, not only for ourselves but for everyone.

With these principles, techniques and methods in hand, let's move now to see how this all comes into practice when it's time to get to work.

PART V
RESEARCH FOUNDATIONS AND LOGISTICS

BUILDING YOUR TEAM

Now it's time to introduce the tactical workings of conducting UX research effectively, using the lens of the Heart of UX teachings and our experiences working as consultants and in-house researchers. This chapter is intended to serve as a fundamental reference you can bookmark and return to often. To accommodate this goal, we're also interspersing helpful checklists for you to use.

Stakeholders: Prime Movers of UX

Stakeholders don't just chase wayward vampires around. They're the people who request and own any UX project. There are lots of good books on how to work with stakeholders of all types, especially on how to garner their buy-in to the UX process. We're not going to cover that. Here we'll be focusing on how to integrate the Heart of UX techniques into your work with stakeholders.

We first need to take the position that stakeholders are a fundamental part of the project. It's at the initial discovery/stakeholder engagement phase that the formulated research questions will determine the shape of the research and ultimately, the outcomes. Stakeholders hold the keys to what the research will focus on, and ultimately, how it will be implemented. As such, we apply the very same relational and inquiry skills that we've been developing for research sessions to our interactions with those involved in the broader project.

Determining the Needs of the Project

It's often the case that a stakeholder will come to you with a specific research method in mind such as, "I want you to run a ten-person usability test on this design." The reflexive approach would have us take the request and execute it, delivering what was asked for, on time and on budget. This is so easy to do in a busy, results-oriented environment where we get over-focused on hitting milestones and goals. Instead of the reflexive yes, this is where we can instead pause, reflect, and start asking deepening questions to see if there's something else that's needed instead that may be of better benefit to the overall UX and success of the project.

Make Sure the Schedule and Scope Make Sense

We also need to ensure we stay resourced enough to be able to perform the research properly. This means not over-promising or exceeding our capacity just to hit a deadline. Research deliverables are not a commodity. We don't measure success in the quantity of findings—it's the quality of findings that matters.

Below are the types of questions you could ask of your stakeholders when they come to you requesting what may seem to be an overly specific type of research.

- Why do they want that many people?
- Are there different types of people?
- Are they looking to make comparisons?
- How will the results of the research be used?
- What would success look like?
- What would failure look like?

By treating your stakeholder interactions as a form of research in its own right, you can ask the kinds of deepening questions you pose to your research participants in order to better understand their needs and motivations. Doing so will help to ensure that your work is valued, useful, and able to be conducted in a way that will respect your capacity.

STUDY PLANNING

Now that you've gained alignment with your stakeholders, it's time to design the scaffolding of your research project. You'll need to determine methods, participants, scope, timing, and outcomes and all of this information goes into the Study Plan.

Everything takes shape with the Study Plan. We can't stress enough how important this step is—skipping it will only lead to peril and tears. Seriously, start with a Study Plan. This is your map for everything that will follow. And it's also a way to ensure that everyone is aligned with the project, from the beginning all the way to the end.

Components of a Study Plan

Below are the basic elements of a Study Plan, with commentary and illustrations. There are of course variations to how these plans are presented and constructed, largely due to the specific needs of a team or audience. What we're presenting are the most essential elements we've found to be of most importance.

Cover Page

Project name

Date

Research Goals

Primary Goal: "Understand what opportunities exist for creating a more engaging type of digital dashboard in self-driving cars."

Secondary Goal: "Determine if people still need a dashboard in a car they can't drive."

These are the desired outcomes of the research. If these goals are achieved, the research project is a success. All components of the Study Plan should serve these goals. If they don't, we should question if they belong within the project. Write these goals as broad, aspirational strokes, the place to get more specific and detailed is to follow in the research questions.

Research Questions

"Do riders want to communicate with the dashboard using voice?"

"What are riders' impressions of the concepts we've developed? Do they find them useful? Engaging? Delightful? If not, why? If yes, what specifically makes them feel that way?"

These questions can get as specific as needed, and you'll likely gather them from different members of the team who have a stake in the research. Keep in mind that developing and using too many questions may mean running out of time during the session. For this reason, it's a good idea to list these in priority order and communicate that to people. If you find that you don't have time to get to everything comfortably within the time allotted, you'll likely need to trim the list of questions. Again, make sure these questions somehow tie in to the research goals.

Participants

"People who may have heard of self-driving cars but have not yet ridden in one as a passenger."

25-34 years old

Tech engaged but not early adopters

Residents of a mid-sized metro, i.e. Bellingham, Washington or Boulder, Colorado

Determining the right participants, as well as the appropriate specificity of their characteristics, are additional factors that can make or break your research study. If you talk to people who are deemed too far away from your target market, stakeholders may cry foul if they don't like the results of the research and claim that you didn't talk to the right people. This is more common than it may seem, and if not properly managed, it can sink an entire project. This is an area of the Study Plan that should garner extra attention and sign-off from your stakeholders, ensuring there is a superabundance of agreement with who has been determined to participate.

Another ditch that's easy to fall into is agreeing to too much specificity with your participants. It can quickly become the case that the target participants are simply too hard to locate, or are too far from reality.

Method

- *"We will begin the 90-minute sessions by conducting an in-person site visit at people's homes and then transitioning to a 45-minute ride in the test vehicle, departing from their home and returning to their home."*

Here's a special note about selecting research methods. The following table gives a brief (and by no means comprehensive) list of common types of research methodologies. It is beyond the scope of this book to fully outline and explore each method, but the salient idea is that knowing the outcome you want maps directly to selecting the appropriate methods, again consider the project goals. In general, the generative/formative methods are best employed during the initial discovery stage of a design process, where we don't always know the product that needs to be developed, or there is a lack of understanding of the desired customer. It's also highly appropriate when determining overall strategy. Validation/summative methods are useful once a product has been designed, or there is a concept or idea to test. Also of note, some of these methods can be both formative and summative.

Generative/Formative	Validation/Summative
Ethnographies/Site Visits	Usability Studies
Grounded Theory (Phenomenological Research)	Closed Card Sorts
Structured Interviews	Tree Testing
Diary Studies	Eye Tracking
Open Card Sorts	Heuristic Evaluations

Tasks:

"Show me how you would direct the car to take you to Whole Foods."

"En route, one of your passengers wants to stop for a coffee. How would you add a stop on the way?"

Employing study tasks are a staple of usability research and can be a double-edged sword. They must be employed with the intention that they are a guide for the research, not a prescription. Too much rigidity in following the flow of the tasks and you're likely to guide the conversation too much in an effort to check the boxes. Too little adherence to the tasks and you risk missing valuable data points that will answer the research questions and serve the study goals.

Part of the art is in knowing when and how to present a task to a participant. This could be a whole chapter in itself, but a good rule of thumb is this: If presenting the task feels forced and artificial to you in your body, then it feels forced to the participant as well. If, on the other hand, you're gently guiding the conversation, you'll naturally find a place to insert the tasks into the thread of the experience.

Again, this takes a great deal of practice to feel natural, and as we've emphasized in previous chapters, it's imperative that the participant feels comfortable in the interaction. People are often willing to go along with forced-choice conversations, such as when responding to a survey, but that's not a path to authentic, alive insights.

Measures

Qualitative:

"Participant feedback provided during 'think-aloud' protocol."

"Spontaneous expressions of frustration, joy, delight, and other salient emotions."

Quantitative:

"Frequency of error and success at tasks."

"Responses to post-session satisfaction metrics."

"Responses to the System Usability Scale"

Stating how things will be measured helps all to understand by which metrics the research will be analyzed, synthesized and ultimately, reported. This book is centered solely on qualitative methods, but often there is a need to mix qualitative measures with quantitative, and doing so can provide additional lenses that are helpful.

> **Other Items to Include**
>
> As stated previously, what we've presented are what we've seen to be the essential bits of a study plan. But there are others that may be of use to your particular environment and project needs:
>
> - Deliverables: outlining specifically how things will be reported.
> - Timing: the project schedule.
> - Assumptions: what will and will not be present in the project, etc.
> - Roles: who will be the study moderator, note-taker, videographer, etc.

Sharing the Study Plan

We like to host a project kick-off meeting, inviting everyone who is involved in the project. We share the study plan, walk through all the sections, and then make any edits in person and on the spot. We tell people at the beginning and end of the meeting that this is exactly the plan we will follow and that this is the time to make any revisions before research begins.

This practice establishes trust and is safety-making for all involved. It also builds a sense of partnership and co-creation around the research.

Best Practices for Study Planning

Be flexible and have an experimental attitude—nothing ever goes completely according to plan. Be willing to try something and then change it if need be, depending on the course of the project and what you're seeing from the field and the conversations you are having.

Take the time to clarify your purpose, resources, and desired outcome. Ask yourself, "With these current resources, what is the best possible outcome?" Ask stakeholders the same question. Know your limits, but aim for the stars.

Claim your bias. Make mind maps, brainstorm, and hold brain dump sessions to identify assumptions, hypothesis, known biases. Take on the mindset of the intentional observer.

Consider budget, scope, audience, and timeline. Work backwards, understanding the desired deliverable. Do you need a high fidelity video, or a comprehensive presentation of findings? Or would a simple document be best?

MODERATOR'S GUIDES

The purpose of the moderator's guide is to reflect the goals and methods of the study plan and keep us on track while research is underway. It's a portable reference with all of the notes, probes, and pointers that the research team needs while in the field. It's typically not shared with the client or stakeholders due to its technical, applied nature, although some will want to at least see it.

Seen through the lens of the Heart of UX, the Moderator's Guide enables us to maintain our focus on the participant, environment and interactions, as opposed to thinking too much about the logistics and particulars of conducting the research.

Components of a Moderator's Guide

Again, formats vary widely, and they should. This guide is for you, the researcher, and only you know what's going to work best for your particular style. We've noted that our guides have become more and more essential and streamlined across projects, existing mostly as bullet lists so that they can be quickly scanned only when needed, in order to maintain as much connection and attention with the participants as possible.

In constructing your guide, a good rule of thumb is to start with the Study Plan as a template and then trim it down to only what is necessary. Then add in the notes you'll need in the field.

Here's a basic starting point for some components of such a guide.

Session Setup Reminders

Compensation: $175 via Venmo or PayPal

Open Slack channel for in-session questions with stakeholders

Test set-up: (ex. reset the prototype between participants)

Start screen share recording

Participant Orientation

Orient them to the session environment, cameras, and format. This is just as important to do when sessions are remote as it is in person.

Discuss logistics such as timing, parking validation, restrooms, and taking breaks.

Tasks/Interview Questions

Be sure to add probes and follow up questions on your guide, in case your brain is tired and there's a lull in the conversation, or you're not sure where to go next.

Concluding Discussion

"What did you like most?"

"What did you like least?"

"If you could tell the designers one thing to improve, what would it be?"

Wrap Up

Payment details

Sincere thanks for their time, presence, and participation

CONDUCTING RESEARCH SESSIONS

At the Start of Each Research Day: Cultivating the Curious Witness

Here is a Heart of UX checklist to scan before a day of interviewing. The Connected Researcher in practice is always purposefully re-aligning with their own intention, checking their orientation, and staying curious.

- Don't fixate on what you expect to learn, but rather cultivate your own general, non-specific curiosity.
- Intend to build rapport. Be courteous, interested, kind, and focus on the aliveness in the person.
- Ask questions, especially deepening questions as possible. Your choice of questions and how you offer them shows how intently you are listening.
- Be mindful of body language. Your body is communicating, and so is theirs. You can contact body language to show that you are listening. "Feeling tired, huh?"
- Employ mindfulness to be present with whatever is happening. "Life as it is."
  - Accept people as they are.
  - Accept what's happening in each moment.
  - Allowing is not the same as passivity. Keep your curiosity on board.

Before Starting Each Session— Pre-Session Checklist

Every pilot, no matter how experienced, conducts a pre-flight check and uses a checklist. The reason for this is that all of us, at any time, can forget something or something may have changed with your equipment that you're not aware of.

There is also value in ensuring you're in the proper space: mentally, emotionally, and somatically, prior to entering the field of a session with another person where all things are possible.

To make sure you are personally prepared for moderation:

- Have your note-taking supplies ready.
- Have your moderator's guide printed or available on a screen.
- Have water and tissues on hand.
- Take care of your own basic needs: Go to the restroom, have a snack, and so forth.
- Have back-ups:
  - Back-up recording equipment, Internet access, another version of the prototype, etc.
  - A colleague available in case of session questions or unforeseen circumstances with the participant.

After these items have been satisfied, make sure you have between three to five minutes available to sit in silence. Check in with your body. Follow your breath. Close your eyes if you like. Acknowledge that you are about to meet a fellow human being who may be nervous, not knowing what to expect and that they will be looking to you to know what to do and how to be.

This person has their own unique story to tell you. And, as the popular saying goes, each person may be fighting their own individual battle at that moment. This is an opportunity for them to have 45, 60, or 90 minutes of your full attention. They may have never experienced an attuned person such as yourself before now. This time could be a gift to another human being who needs your presence and unconditional positive regard in that moment. All the while you are serving the needs of the project simply by actively fostering feelings of appreciation for whomever this person may be.

Participant Orientation

As we've stressed, orientation is of prime importance to participant comfort and trust in you, the researcher. Below are some guidelines on how you can orient each person at the start of each session:

- Give the person a moment to look around the room if you they are meeting with you in-person and in a new space. Point out a feature, like an interesting picture or light in order to give them tacit permission to do so.

- Go over the session details—such as the length and purpose of the session.
- Set the pace of the conversation from the very beginning. Your cadence, attunement, and attitude all determine how the session will go from here.
- Allow this orientation to be for you also. Orient to the person, take a breath, and get into a rhythm with them and their unique expression.

The following is an example of an orienting script that you may choose to include for your Moderator's Guide.

Overview

First thing, thanks for your help today. Before we get started, I am going to give you a quick overview of what to expect. I am [name]. I'm a user researcher. This session will take up to an hour. Feel free to take a break whenever you need to.

You're going to be working with a couple of devices today and setting them up. This desk is for you to use. All of the equipment on it is available to you, and you can just imagine that this is your home desk.

I'll simply be observing you as you explore these devices, asking some questions along the way about your experience. I may ask you to slow down or pause at certain points to ask these questions. I'd like to emphasize that there's no right or wrong way to do anything, and there's nothing specific that I'm looking for. I'm just here to understand your experiences.

I've had nothing to do with the creation of the devices that you'll be using, so nothing you say will hurt my feelings. Please give me your candid feedback, whether that's positive or negative. Also please talk me through any thoughts or reactions that you're having to what you're seeing.

(Note: this is a lot of information, so check for understanding at this point to see if they have questions.)

> ### More Details
>
> *When we're done, you will receive your compensation. You will need to sign to acknowledge that you received it.*
>
> *I have some co-workers observing this session, but it will be just you and I talking today. I'm also recording our conversation so that I don't have to take so many notes while we talk. Do you have any questions?*
>
> ### Optional: Introducing a Prototype
>
> *Today we will be working with a new design idea. We call this a prototype—it's like a blueprint. You may see that it does not have very many colors, styles, or pictures. You may also notice that some text is placeholder text, just to show you where text might be. We will be focused on organization and layout, and how it would work best to suit your needs, rather than the look and feel of the website. Please use your imagination and share your ideas with us to create the best version of this new idea.*
>
> (Format the orientation to fit your specific needs, just be sure to convey that none of this is an evaluation of them and that you're going to be present with them the whole time.)

After Ending Each Session—Post-Session Debrief and Release

It is a common, valuable practice to debrief with your team after each session. Take at least a few minutes to confer on what was noticed, evaluations of the prototype, if any, or task performance. What is often not noted in these discussions, however, is the emotional, limbic impact the person had on the researcher and observers. This is important primary data. Remember, our bodies and minds are the most sophisticated instruments ever imagined, especially in relation to other bodies and minds—and we don't want to let that information go unacknowledged.

In addition to a more factual debrief with your team, try asking each other deepening questions, such as:

- "What was the thing you found most inspiring about this person?"
- "Were there any challenges you personally resonated with or had an impact on you?"
- "What do you think would help this person feel the most joy they've ever experienced?"

The answers to these questions could be empathy-building, or they may just be funny. "They were yawning the whole time and seemed checked out. I think they would most like a hammock and a beer on the beach." Whatever comes up, the point is to help encourage seeing this person as they are, in that moment. Experiment with your own debrief discussion questions that feel most alive for you.

In addition to the debrief, it's also of value to you as the researcher to fully release this person before you meet with the next one, or even more importantly, before you end your day and go home or go out for the night. Doing so frees your system up to be a finely calibrated measurement instrument and also allows you to recenter back into your own experience.

Cleaning up and filing away any notes, recordings, etc. from this session is a good embodied practice of releasing that person. You may also wish to have a silent ritual in your mind as you actively release and say goodbye to this person that you may have had a meaningful connection with.

VIDEO AND THE HEART OF UX

The impact of an artfully placed video on a report's delivery cannot be overstated. People who may have been checking-out during a presentation suddenly pay attention. Done right, the message goes deep and gets the point across. Before you know it, the video is being shared all around the company and people are talking about it. It is used in executive presentations to get a point across, to convince, to persuade, and build empathy.

This is a dreamy situation for researchers: to have this level of impact, reach, and uptake with your findings. There's definitely an elegance to accomplishing this, conveying video in a way that elicits maximal impact in as little time possible. There's an ethical consideration to this as well, a responsibility to use this influential ability sparingly so as to keep the dignity of the person of focus as a priority. For these reasons, we're going to take a comprehensive dive into this subject that is often considered an afterthought.

Embracing the Camera

Before we get into production of that beautiful and impactful video, we should begin with an unconventional focus on the camera itself.

The camera is a central and yet often-overlooked component of the work we do. It's how we capture sessions: for analysis, fact-checking, and sharing. Most of us have a strained relationship with cameras. When they're brought out and placed before us, we change. Notice this next time it happens—we get self-conscious, we smile, we pose.

Why do we change? Because we've suddenly become acutely self-focused and self-aware. But this awareness is a projection outside of ourselves. In that moment, we're picturing the future judgment of seeing ourselves. The judgment of others seeing us. This is why we want to pose, to look good, look happy. We want to convey an image of ourselves that may or may not actually be us in that moment, because to see ourselves as we really are, at this very moment, can be difficult.

We don't tend to see cameras coming out during difficult times in our lives. We don't take pictures in the middle of our divorce, during the death of a loved one, or our bankruptcy. We reserve the cameras for vacations, concerts, or graduations.

Consider that for your research participant in that moment, they may see this as a potentially embarrassing event, their struggle with technology in front of a person who's watching them, complete with a live-streaming camera.

It's our assertion that in order for you, as a Connected Researcher, to compassionately include a camera in your research interactions, you must also do some work around your own relationship with the camera.

What you may discover is that the camera is much more than a tool for recording. It can also be a tool for seeing differently, understanding differently, and seeing one another more deeply.

Try this practice with a partner:

- Get a camera that can record audio and video. If in person, place it between yourself and another, positioned so that it's going to provide a mostly face-on view of the subject. This means that for the interviewer, the camera will be roughly eye level and just out of the line of vision. If you're doing this remotely, position the webcam so that it's roughly at your eye level.

- Choose who wants to be the interviewer and who wants to be interviewed. Now both of you pause to notice anything that may have arisen around what it was like to have made that choice. What does this point to with respect to your camera comfort? You may feel ready to be doing the filming or more comfortable being the one on camera. Both of these orientations are information.

- Now open up a timer and then for five minutes, interview your subject about something interesting to them while you record them with the camera. Have them speak about something interesting and alive. Ask them to describe their most recent trip, or perhaps a recent noteworthy event in their lives.

- As you record them, notice how it feels in your body to know that this conversation is being recorded. How does this shift your experience of this person? Do you notice yourself interacting differently than you would without the camera? Are you hesitant to say what you think, or are you instead suddenly much more chatty than before? Take a mental note of these events as they occur.

- When the five minutes are over, both of you close your eyes and sit across from one another for thirty seconds. Take any quick notes you'd like, and then without debriefing, switch roles so the storyteller is now the interviewer.
- After another five minutes, sit for thirty seconds again and notice your sensations. Take quick notes and then talk to each other. What was that like? What did you notice? Did you forget the camera was there in the connection? Was it so distracting you couldn't focus?

What did you learn from this experience?

How do you feel now about the idea of watching that video of yourself?

How do you feel about watching the video of the other person?

You might discuss the answers to these questions with your partner if you wish. You may find that you see this person or yourself in a different light than you did before. The camera has a unique ability to greatly enhance the amount of visual and auditory information and the subconscious knows this. It is why many people are nervous around them. As you're ostensibly recording people as a component of your research, we feel it's our responsibility to experience this in order to cultivate compassion for our participants' experience so that we may take appropriate steps to help them feel more at ease.

If and when you feel resourced to do so, you can take the next step by watching your video, the recording of you being interviewed. But let's do this in the most discerning way possible by following this technique. You're about to watch the video of yourself.

- Put on headphones.
- Find a quiet spot where you feel comfortable, and far away enough to feel like it's just you, and you can't feel the judgment of anyone else watching. It's just you and you.
- Before you watch the video, close your eyes and think of someone you love and have great care for. Maybe your child, your partner, your grandmother,

- your dog, someone you feel could do no wrong. Notice this feeling of unconditional love and appreciation.
- Take this feeling with you as you view this video of yourself. Actively cultivate the feelings of loving presence, appreciation, and compassion and extend those feelings to the being you see before you. This is a person worthy of your love, care, and full attention.
- After you've watched some or all of the video, you might reflect on how the experience affected how you view and feel about yourself.

After facilitating people through this experience, we often witness something transformational as one feels a sense of compassion for themselves that they were not previously aware of. This may not happen right away, or ever. There's a lot of self-criticism present for most of us, after all, but it occurs often enough that this seems worth doing.

Now that you've had this personal, embodied experience of the potency of the camera, you may find yourself extending compassion and empathy toward the people you see on your video file—and perhaps there are ways to convey this same empathy with those who you present it to.

VIDEO MASTERY IN QUALITATIVE RESEARCH

We won't go into a full discussion of videography techniques, only discussing here what seems essential to the practice of UX research. Why is this important? Because we're not just doing research, we're engaging in connected, attuned research, and this is evocative stuff. When people are expressing things like heartfelt desires, motivations, and authentic emotions, we want to be able to faithfully convey these events to observers and stakeholders and do so in a way that will add to the credibility of our message.

There are four primary contexts where we as researchers often find ourselves recording video. But before we get into specifics, there are two universal and often overlooked ways that time and again we've seen degrade the quality of a recording: audio and lighting.

Great audio will help you make a lasting impact with your video clips. Bad audio is irritating, hard to connect with, and will make clips seem amateur, negatively impacting your credibility and your ability to get your message across.

Lighting paints the overall tone: glaring fluorescent light from above is harsh and this harshness will carry through to the video. Light from behind a person makes their image dim and their faces hard to see.

We'll touch on the nuances and best practices of lighting and audio further as we discuss each of the below contexts. We also provide guidance on the position of your body relative to your environment and the participants you're working with.

Remote Research

Conducting remote research sessions is one of our favorite methods, for a few reasons.

- We can talk to people from all over the world without needing to go anywhere. This greatly extends our reach and capabilities.
- People are often more comfortable speaking with us as they're in their own environments.
- We benefit from the ethnographic bonus of seeing people's homes, offices, etc. as well as their computer desktop, mobile apps, and so forth, when they share their screens with us.

Despite these benefits, video can be more complex to do well in a remote context. A major complicating factor is the fact that we have no control over the participants' setup. They may join your meeting with premium sound and a high-definition camera, or be using their computer's microphone and built in camera with dark lighting. In this case, the only thing we can really control is our half of the conversation. The following guidelines are tried-and-true based on thousands of hours of conducting remote research sessions using a wide array of online conferencing platforms. Following these will lead to videos that are just as engaging as anything taking place in person.

Video

The high-definition camera and multi-use microphone are again what we will recommend in this environment, as well as a high-bandwidth connection as we are fully dependent on the quality of the connection to maintain resonance with our participants.

Place the camera so that it is as close to the top edge of the screen as possible and as close to eye level as possible in order to facilitate as close of an approximation to eye contact as possible. This may necessitate your conducting remote sessions from a standing desk orientation, or otherwise positioning the camera and desk to achieve this effect. If not, the video has you peering down at the person you're speaking with.

When you're speaking with the participant, try to keep your eyes as close to the camera as possible in order to maintain relative eye contact. Even looking somewhere else on the screen for only what feels like a small amount of time has a large effect on the interaction. One technique that we've found effective is to place the online meeting window as close to the webcam as possible. This helps you keep your face and eyes oriented as closely to the participants' as you can.

If you're conducting remote sessions from a large room, a conference room for example, you may be used to dialing in using the room camera. This has a distancing effect on the interaction, however and this is not recommended for this reason. Instead, use the webcam and position it close to yourself, as you would in any other environment.

These may seem like extraneous details, but we recommend trying it out to see the difference in the conversation. You may be surprised at the great effects of these minor adjustments.

Audio

You'll want to use headphones if you can so that you can hear your participants more clearly. Most quality headphones also now provide at least acceptable audio microphones as well.

You may wish to instead use a higher quality microphone if you want podcast-quality audio. We recommend a microphone that allows you to set a specific polar pattern.

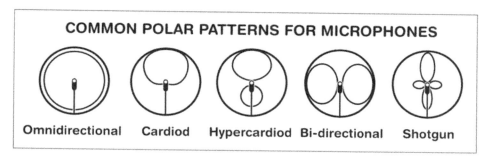

Set the gain level. You can think of the gain like the volume on headphones or speakers except in reverse: it's the level the mic will use to record. Too much gain, and your audio will "clip"—it will exceed the capacity of the microphone and get distorted, sometimes so much as to be unintelligible. With too little gain, the audio is faint.

For remote research setups, set your microphone to shotgun mode, as it's just your audio being captured.

Positioning

We've already discussed the importance of keeping your camera at eye-level. Another factor to consider is your background and lighting. So many remote conversations take place with someone's dark kitchen with a slowly rotating ceiling fan in the background. Trust us, this is distracting and ruins the mood. Be mindful of what is behind you. Ideally there's a nice wall or bookshelf you can place behind you. If you have a beautiful view and window behind you, that's great, but be sure to fill your light in front of you with an added light source, so that you're not a dark silhouette with a beach scene behind you.

If you don't have a nice background available, consider a small investment in a backdrop. A simple white background, or even a tasteful patterned background, goes a long way with overcoming any effects that an otherwise distracting room may have on the conversation.

The position of your attention

A final note about positioning in remote meetings. This one is subtle, but it has to do with the position of your attention. It's very easy to get distracted in an online conversation. It may be your third session of the day and you're not really feeling the conversation. You might be tempted to glance at that email, or check those Slack notifications that keep bouncing in your dock. As much as you can, resist the urge to peek at your other windows or interact with others during your call.

Although it seems like they don't, the other person notices when you peek at a distraction, especially if you've already attuned with them and have established Unconditional Positive Regard. They'll feel your attention drop and know that you're not paying attention. This situation is recoverable, of course, but it's important to know that dropping attention has an impact on the interaction.

The in-person Usability Lab

Let's assume a very common, standard setup in the usability lab. Someone is seated next to you and they're being asked to interact with a prototype on a computer screen or mobile device. For this scenario, thankfully the tech required to do this well is very approachable. All one needs is a way to record/live share the desktop, the video of the participant, and capture quality audio of the conversation:

- Recording of the desktop and live sharing is accomplished using an online conferencing platform.

- Video of the participant is captured using a tripod and a premium quality webcam—preferably one that supports HD video or similar for crisp, engaging images.

- If you're also capturing video of a mobile device, you can add a second camera in the form of a quality document camera. We've found these cameras to be incredibly versatile, as they can also be used in participatory design exercises done on paper, working with hardware devices, or any other scenario where you wish to see what a person is doing with their hands.

- Instead of relying on the small microphones found on the computer or the webcam, we recommend a dedicated, high quality desktop microphone. There are many readily available that offer superb sound quality and versatility at a very reasonable price.

Now that you've got your equipment, it's time to set up the space in the lab. There are a myriad of different configurations, but we'll present some that have worked well for us. You may wish to start with these initial setups and experiment with what works best for you and your particular needs and constraints. You'll notice that these configurations have you occupying the same space as the participant, not seated behind glass.

But first, before you jump in, just look at the room. Where does it seem you'll both be most comfortable? Where will the lighting be most optimal? Consider how you'd like to orient before placing the equipment.

1. **Positioning Side by Side**

In this configuration, you're sitting roughly right next to the participant. You'll have your body angled so as to be as open to them as possible so you can have a

comfortable conversation, but you will also wish to see what they're doing and be able to take intermittent notes if needed.

Video

Place the camera on a tripod and set it on the desk, roughly between you and the participant, with the camera lens facing them. This may seem counterintuitive as you may think to place the webcam where they typically go, on top of the screen, but this video angle is actually quite awkward from the viewer's vantage, with lots of time seeing someone looking down or their forehead.

A more intimate and compelling video is accomplished with the side-on face shot that is made available with the camera between you. Set the tripod height approximately at eye level. This conveys a feeling of conversing with someone in a manner we're all accustomed to with eyes more directly in line with ours.

Audio

Place the microphone roughly between the both of you but far enough back on the desk so it's not in your way. For this side by side configuration, you'll want the cardioid pattern, as you'll both be next to one another.

Practice sitting in the facilitator and participants' seats and talking to see what audio gain setting is best for this environment.

2. **Positioning across from one another**

This configuration also works well in the lab and may be easier on your body for prolonged periods, as you're not needing to twist your torso to face the participant while also attending to your screen. There are a couple of accommodations to be made to make this work. One of them is that you'll now be looking at your own computer screen to view the video feed and see what they're doing with whatever you're working with.

This has some advantages, one of them being that now you're seeing what your viewers are seeing, as well as what's on the resultant video file. You'll be much more likely to spot something that may need adjustment, like maybe the mobile device is slightly off camera and needs to be placed in a better position to have a better view.

This configuration also allows you to position your laptop out of view of the participant and enables you to chat or Slack with others on your team without fear of the conversation catching the person's eye.

It also places the video camera directly in front of the person's face, which is why this arrangement is an optimal option. The video captures all of the facial nuances possible, while they speak with you and also as they work with the computer or device.

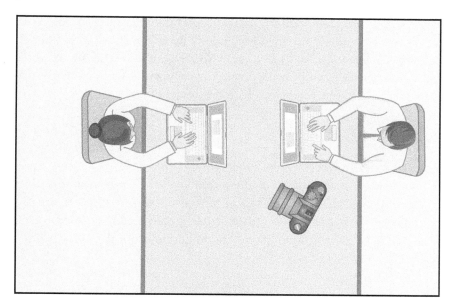

For this arrangement, place the microphone between you and set the pattern to hypercardioid or shotgun, keeping in mind that there are some trade-offs for each option and you'll want to experiment to see which is best for you.

In The Field/On Location

Shooting video in the field and on location is rich with the prospect of capturing something amazing and compelling, something no one has ever seen before. It's also technically challenging, as you won't have the luxury of as much control over the environment as you would in a fixed environment like the usability lab. Most of the time, we have only a few moments to get the camera and audio situated before we begin the session, so practicing with these principles will certainly help.

Video

Video captured in the field can take a few different approaches, largely depending on your comfort level with cameras. The simplest approach is to purchase a video camera, drop it on your tripod and go. A downside to this is having all those large video files on an SD card that then needs to get placed somewhere, organized and dealt with. With experience and a good system in place, this certainly becomes workable.

Another option is to use your webcam and laptop as the recording device. This keeps everything in one place and means you don't need to work with additional equipment and can just focus on the research. You'll want to be mindful of your disk capacity, as video files can be quite large. You may wish to move video to an external hard drive between sessions to keep this under control.

Audio

Audio becomes even more of a focus on field visits as you often won't know what kinds of noises and volumes you'll encounter until you get there and start setting up. We've found that in this case, it helps to have two different types of microphones: a microphone that allows for customizable patterns such as shotgun and omnidirectional; or a shotgun mic, maybe the same one from the lab, with the second being a lavalier mic.

The lavalier mic has some great advantages in a loud environment. It clips on a person's clothing and is placed near and facing their mouth. Even in a very loud coffee shop, for example, you'll be able to hear their words loud and clear. The only detriment to a lavalier mic is that your part of the conversation will not be captured. This can be solved with a second lavalier mic, but that also adds more complexity to your setup, so you may decide it's not necessary.

Positioning

You'll find that this is a place where your flexibility and ingenuity can really pay off. If you can, position the video of your participant so that the background and surroundings reflect the uniqueness and tone of the place. Imagine your participant is the owner of a high end auto mechanics shop and you're there to discuss something relevant to running a small business. Most of us have never been in such an environment, certainly not from the perspective beyond the waiting room. In this case, the owner may think to conduct the interview in their office at the back of the shop.

But what if you could instead talk somewhere near the action, position the perfect shot so that the owner is the central focus and the cars and tools and lifts and busy mechanics are the background? How much more compelling would this be to your clients and stakeholders?

Try to position your camera as close to your face and at your eye level as possible in order to imbue the resultant video with a sense of speaking with a person face to face.

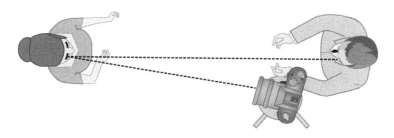

It is not always possible to get such compositions, but our point to convey to you is to consider it and see what is possible. Consider how you can best capture the feel and uniqueness of the place in order to help tell your story.

In Focus Groups

Focus groups offer you more control over your environment, as with a usability lab, but they also have the added challenge of many more people. Not to worry, however, this is easily mitigated with the right approach.

You'll find a great deal of variety with the kinds of video/audio possibilities at focus group facilities. They often provide their own built-in cameras and microphones for you to use. But in our experience these are not typically of the best quality devices, and they tend to be offered at too great a cost. We prefer to bring in our own equipment in these situations.

Video

We've had a great deal of success using either a standalone video camera or a webcam plus a computer. Again, both offer advantages and disadvantages. The webcam offers simplicity but lacks the optical zoom capacity of a standalone video camera. You may wish to use a standalone if you have a particularly compelling moment/speaker in your group.

Whichever you choose, we recommend placing the camera on a tripod on the table near the moderator. This again affords a camera view with participants facing the camera, as well as allowing for panning as needed to capture individuals around the room as they speak. If you keep the zoom fairly wide, you'll be able to see something like half the group at one time and this will minimize the need for too much panning.

Audio

Audio in a focus group is fairly straightforward. In this situation, you'll want an omnidirectional microphone, or to place your customizable microphone in omnidirectional mode. This spreads the recording pattern around the room in a 360-degree audio capture. You may wish to keep a closer eye on the gain levels and do some testing before the group begins, as you'll need to account for people who are loud talkers, soft talkers, and medium talkers. Getting the gain right is important.

Positioning

For the sake of the video recording of groups, and live feeds, you'll want to position yourself relative to the group so that the one-way glass (if present) is not behind the group. Otherwise you'll inevitably see the camera and microphone in the shot. This positioning has the moderator with the glass behind them. It also benefits any observers behind the glass, as people will be then speaking in their direction.

Of course, one does not need to be in a focus group facility to conduct a focus group. Any large room will do just fine, and observers will then be able to view the session via video.

Part V: Research Foundations and Logistics

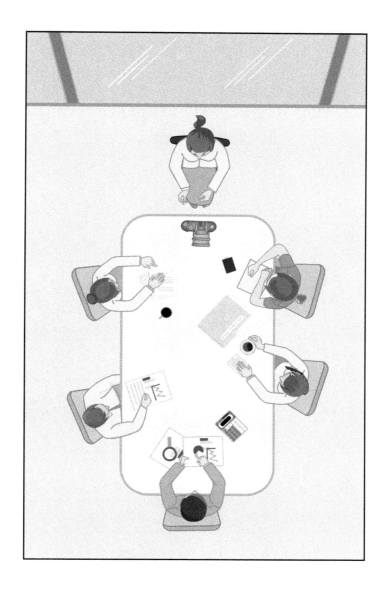

A FINAL WORD

A Final Word

The principles and techniques presented in this book provide a tangible path to balance the very real demands of UX research jobs with our ability to thrive and connect with others. These connections lead directly to deeper insights and serve to fuel our creativity through common humanity.

The Heart of UX is a call for all of us to advance our craft as human-centric explorers, and turn toward our experiences as people in bodies. This enables us to do the same for our research participants and experience truly embodied empathy.

In parallel with the incredible advances that continue to take place in technology, there have also been remarkable advances in the practice of User Experience Research. Even in the era of COVID-19 and the resultant need to do more of our relational work remotely, we have been able to reach people in ways never before possible using an astonishing array of tools and platforms.

What we hope to see as a part of our next wave of professional evolution are further advances of the heart, self-care, compassion, and of consciousness.

ACKNOWLEDGMENTS

To our families—thank you for giving us a solid foundation upon which to grow. Together we are all both the rock and the tree.

To our teachers—Flint, Peg, Gregory, James, and Rupesh—overflowing thanks for giving us the ability to see, feel and be truly ourselves.

To our amazing, inspiring daughter, Emily Mae—we live our fullest life because of you. Thank you for choosing us as your parents.

To countless others, through all time and space, for the support, interest, encouragement, and motivation.

To our editor, Ron, without whom this book would not have happened.

To the readers, who get something out of this offering and make it their own.

ABOUT THE AUTHORS

Jessica Steinbomer

As a researcher, teacher, and facilitator with over 20 years of experience in the field of UX Research, Jessica leads workshops, trainings and retreats that focus on connection and work-life balance to bring whole person wellness to the UX industry. Jessica utilizes her analytical perspective as a researcher and co-owner of Progress UX Research, merged with her extensive training in body based therapies like yoga and somatic psychology to facilitate integration of mind and body for both the person and the business. Jessica helps client teams integrate best practices of health merged with best practices for business to support creative professionals.

Jon-Eric Steinbomer

Jon-Eric has worked in the field of UX Research since 1999. As a consultant for most of his career, he has worked with a uniquely broad array of companies, primarily in the technology sector. He has helped form experiences for an equally diverse range of technologies: robotics, home automation, self-driving cars, e-commerce websites, apps, and services. He considers his approach to UX Research to be built upon three pillars:

- A love of people
- A desire to tell their stories
- A drive to innovate how research is done

Jon-Eric's approach has been greatly influenced by his studies and practice of Hakomi, a somatic psychotherapy based in mindfulness, as well as his ever-unfolding practice of Zen.

NOTES

1. The Hakomi Institute Website, hakomiinstitute.com: The Hakomi Principles

2. The Hakomi Institute Website, hakomiinstitute.com: The Hakomi Method

3. Siegel, Daniel J. *Mindsight: The New Science of Personal Transformation* (New York: Random House Publishing Group, 2010), 26.

4. F. D. Farrow, Tom, and W. R. Woodruff, Peter. *Empathy in Mental Illness* (Cambridge: Cambridge University Press, 2007), 51, 313–314.

5. Kosfeld, M., Heinrichs, M., Zak, P. et al, "Oxytocin Increases Trust in Humans." *Nature* 435 (2005): 673–676. doi:10.1038/nature03701.

6. Seybold, K. S., P. C. Hill, J. K. Neumann, & D. S. Chi, "Physiological and Psychological Correlates of Forgiveness." *Journal of Psychology and Christianity* 20 (2001): 250–259.

7. Regulation of the Neural Circuitry of Emotion by Compassion Meditation: Effects of Meditative Expertise. Lutz, A., J. Brefczynski-Lewis, T. Johnstone, R. J. Davidson, "Regulation of the Neural Circuitry of Emotion by Compassion Meditation: *Effects of Meditative Expertise.*" *PLOS One* 3, no. 3 (2008): e1897.

8. Flow: The Psychology of Optimal Experience—By Mihaly Csikszentmihalyi, page 58

9. Limb C. J., and A. R. Braun, "Neural substrates of spontaneous musical performance: An fMRI study of jazz improvisation." *PLOS One* 3, no. 2 (2008): e1679. https://doi.org/10.1371/journal.pone.0001679.

10. Cameron, O. G., *Visceral Sensory Neuroscience: Interception* (New York: Oxford University Press, 2002).

11. Armour, J. A., "Anatomy and Function of the Intrathoracic Neurons Regulating the Mammalian Heart." in *Reflex Control of the Circulation*, ed. I. H. Zucker and J. P. Gilmore. (Boca Raton: CRC Press, 1991), 1–37.

12. Damasio, A., *Looking for Spinoza: Joy, Sorrow, and the Feeling Brain* (Orlando: Harcourt, 2003).

13. The HeartMath Institute Website, heartmath.org : The Quick Coherence® Technique for Adults.

14. Lambert, Nathaniel M., Steven M. Graham, Frank D. Fincham and Tyler F. Stillman, "A Changed Perspective: How Gratitude Can Affect Sense of Coherence Through Positive Reframing." *Journal of Positive Psychology*, 4, no. 6 (2009): 461–470, doi: 10.1080/17439760903157182.

15. Armour, J. A., "Potential Clinical Relevance of the 'Little Brain' on the Mammalian Heart." *Experimental Physiology* 93, no. 2 (2008): 165–176.

16. Wong, Y. Joel, Jesse Owen, Nicole T. Gabana, Joshua W. Brown, Sydney McInnis, Paul Toth, and Lynn Gilman, "Does Gratitude Writing Improve the Mental Health of Psychotherapy Clients? Evidence from a Randomized Controlled Trial," *Psychotherapy Research* 28, no. 2 (2018): 192–202. doi: 10.1080/10503307.2016.1169332.

17. McCraty, R., and M. Atkinson, "Resilience Training Program Reduces Physiological and Psychological Stress in Police Officers." *Global Advances in Health and Medicine* 1, no. 5: 44–66. doi:10.7453/gahmj.2012.1.5.013.

18. Baule, G., and R. McFee, "Detection of the Magnetic Field of the Heart." *American Heart Journal* 55, no. 7 (1963): 95–96.

19. McCraty, R., et al. The Electricity of Touch: Detection and Measurement of Cardiac Energy Exchange Between People. In *The Fifth Appalachian Conference on Neurobehavioral Dynamics: Brain and Values*. 1996. Radford VA: Lawrence Erlbaum Associates, Inc. Mahwah, NJ.

20. Morris, S. M., "Facilitating Collective Coherence: Group Effects on Heart Rate Variability Coherence and Heart Rhythm Synchronization." *Alternative Therapies in Health and Medicine* 16, no. 4 (2010): 62–72.

21. Susan David, Ph.D. website, susandavid.com: About Emotional Agility, The Book

22. Jha, A. P., A. B. Morrison, J. Dainer-Best, et al., "Minds "At Attention": Mindfulness Training Curbs Attentional Lapses in Military Cohorts." *PLOS One*. https://doi.org/10.1371/journal.pone.0116889.

NOTES

23. The Developing Mind, Second Edition: How Relationships and the Brain Interact to Shape Who We Are, page 19.

24. Manoj K. Bhasin, Denninger, John W., Huffman, Jeff C., Joseph, Marie G., Niles, Halsey, Chad-Friedman, Emma, Goldman, Roberta, Buczynski-Kelley, Beverly, Mahoney, Barbara A., Fricchione, Gregory L., Dusek, Jeffery A., Benson, Herbert, Zusman, Randall M., and Libermann, Towia A, "Specific Transcriptome Changes Associated with Blood Pressure Reduction in Hypertensive Patients After Relaxation Response Training." *The Journal of Alternative and Complementary Medicine* 24, no. 5 (2018): 486–504.

25. Siegel, Daniel, *Aware: The Science and Practice of Presence—The Groundbreaking Meditation Practice*, (New York: Penguin Publishing Group, 2018), 6.

26. Tara Brach, PhD. website, tarabrach.com: Radical Acceptance.

27. Kristin Neff, PhD. "Self-compassion: An Alternative Conceptualization of a Healthy Attitude Toward Oneself." *Self and Identity*, 2, no. 2 (2003), 85–101.

28. Stryker, Rod. *The Four Desires: Creating a Life of Purpose, Happiness, Prosperity, and Freedom*. (New York: Random House Publishing Group, 2011), 137.

29. Erskine, R. G. "Inquiry, Attunement, and Involvement in the Psychotherapy of Dissociation." *Transactional Analysis Journal* 23, no. 4 (1993): 184–190.

30. https://www.heartmath.org/gci/research/global-coherence/

31. Barstow, Cedar. *Right Use of Power: The Heart of Ethics* (New York: Many Realms Publication, 2008).

32. Losada, Marcial, and Emily Heaphy, "The Role of Positivity and Connectivity in the Performance of Business Teams: A Nonlinear Dynamics Model." *American Behavioral Scientist* 47, no. 6 (February 2004): 740–765. doi:10.1177/0002764203260208.

33. Buehlman, K. T., John Gottman, L. F. Katz, "How a Couple Views Their Past Predicts Their Future: Predicting Divorce from an Oral History Interview." *Journal of Family Psychology* 5 no. 3–4: 295–318.

34. Nelson-Isaacs, Sky, *Living in Flow: The Science of Synchronicity and How Your Choices Shape Your World* (New York: North Atlantic Books, 2019), 10.

CPSIA information can be obtained
at www.ICGtesting.com
Printed in the USA
LVHW051204050222
710251LV00016B/926